COMMITTED UNTO US

The Stuckenbrucks' Story

Dedicated to:

Earl Lee, Jane, Dale & Loren.

COMMITTED UNTO US

The

Stuckenbrucks'

Story

By
Ottie Mearl Stuckenbruck

Edited By
Trudy Harvey Tait

Ottie Mearl Stuckenbruck
1603 Woodridge Drive
Johnson City, TN 37604
E-mail: estuckenbruck@yahoo.com

Harvey Christian Publishers, Inc.
449 Hackett Pike, Richmond KY 40475
Tel./Fax (423) 768-2297
E-mail: books@harveycp.com
http://www.harveycp.com

Copyright © 2015
Ottie Mearl Stuckenbruck

All rights reserved. No part of this book may be reproduced or transmitted in any form or by any means, electronic or mechanical, including photocopying, recording, or by any information storage and retrieval system without written permission from the copyright owner, except for the inclusion of brief quotations in a review.

Printed in USA

This Edition 2015

ISBN: 978-1-932774-82-5

Cover Design by
Vlad Vitel
Email: vladyslavvitel@gmail.com

Front cover photograpy by Jackie Schribner
Lower back cover photograph: Tübingen

Printed by
Lightning Source
La Vergne, TN 37086

Contents

Chapter   *Page*

1 Earl's Background, Birth, and Childhood 9
   Earl's Roots on His Father's Side; Earl's Roots on His Mother's Side; Earl's Birth and Childhood; Earl's Teenage and College Years.

2 Ottie Mearl's Background, Birth, and Childhood 26
   Ottie Mearl's Roots on Her Father's Side; Ottie Mearl's Roots on Her Mother's Side; Ottie Mearl's Birth and Childhood; Ottie Mearl's Teenage and College Years.

3 Finding a Life Partner 62
   Ottie Mearl Meets Earl; Wedding Bells.

4 Choosing a Mission 81
   The German Evangelical Association; Dr. Ludwig von Gerdtell.

5 Preparation for Missionary Service in Europe 89
   Getting Started; On the Way; England; Switzerland; Exploring the Possibilities of Germany.

6 Beginning of Our Ministry in Tübingen 103
   Our Introduction to Tübingen; The Proposal; Our First Home and the Birth of Earl Lee; Changes.

7 Furlough (1950-1953) 120
   Home Again and the Birth of Vivian Jane; Fund-raising; Considering the Future.

8 Beginning Our Second Term in Tübingen 131
   Return to Europe, Birth of Dale; Salvaging the Work in Tübingen; Helpers and Visitors; The Holy Land; Temporary Setbacks.

9 The Work Progresses 155
   The Christliche Gemeinde; Dr. Theo Mosalkow; Work Among the Russians; Jane and Earl.

Contents cont.

Chapter   *Page*

10 Other Aspects of the Work 162
      Foreign Professors, Graduate Students, and Fulbright Scolars; The German-American Women's Club; German Customs; Empathy with Those Who Were Seeking a Meaningful Life with Jesus; The Work in Belgum; The Pflegenest (Children's Home); Activities in the Christliche Gemeinde; Conferences and Congresses; Institute for the Study of Christian Origins and the Birth of Loren Theo.

11 Furlough and Final Years in Tübingen 185

12 Adjusting to Life in America 189

13 Tübingen Not Forgotten 194

14 Changes in the Family 198

15 The Work in Tübingen Continues 202

16 Family Matters 206
      An Eventful Year; Earl Retires; Welcome Home Angela from Uruguay; Loren Receives His PhD.; Jane's Journey; Dale; New Arrivals; Awards; Celebrations.

17 At Home and Abroad 230
      Inauguration of the Walker Lectures; Faith in Practice; History of the EES by Some of the Original Cast; EES and Eberhard-Karl Universität Sponser Symposium.

18 Our Family Contracts and Expands 234
      Travels; Farewell to Harry; Earl Released from Earth to His Heavenly Home; Farewell to Earl Lee;

19 Still Walking with Jesus 240
      My Ninetieth Birthday; Into the Future; I Am Ready!

PREFACE

For many years, information about our lives and work, written in diaries, on scraps of paper, in correspondence, and in Christmas letters, cluttered our home. The time came when it was necessary to rid ourselves of this accumulation. In order to preserve at least some of it, I decided to record it for our family. As others, however, read the original manuscript, I was encouraged to make it available to a larger audience.

More than recording the story of our personal lives, I wanted to preserve our commitment as representatives both of the Lord in whose name we served, and of the European Evangelistic Society in Germany. I wished to testify to the presence and guidance of Jesus and the Holy Spirit who undergirded our lives and the lives of those who sent us to accomplish His will.

I owe a big "Thank You" to Dr. Richard Phillips who proofread the story and corrected some of the information. I want to thank my sisters, Gertha Scott and Inell Cochran, and also Peggy Williams for additional information about my early years. I also appreciate Rosemarie Shields for the many hours she spent correcting the material and discussing it with me, and Wilma Buckner for proofreading the document and suggesting how it might be improved. Dr. Calvin and Nancy Ross graciously gave it one final proofing at short notice which I appreciate greatly. I am especially grateful to Trudy Harvey Tait for editing my story. She is the author of six books herself and has been of invaluable help with this manuscript.

In this book you will learn to know us and our family. You will meet people who came together to make it possible for us to serve in Germany and in the States. You will meet others with whom we worked overseas and learn about the Institute for

Research in Christian Origins and the International Christian Church—"faith in practice."

The Tübingen story did not end when my husband and I left Germany. It is ongoing, and, as the years unfold, I hope those who followed us to Tübingen will tell their stories just as I have done.

INTRODUCTION

World War 1 was raging in 1916, the year of Earl Roy Stuckenbruck's birth into a small farming community in Iowa. By the time I was born five years later in Alabama, the war had ended and everyone was looking forward to helping build a new world. For a while, the mood of the country was extremely upbeat. The League of Nations had put together polices to assure us that the war which had just ended would be labeled in the history books as a "war to end all wars." One could not know then, however, that the Great Depression and another World War would take place during the twentieth century.

In the meantime, I met Earl Roy and it soon became evident that we were meant for each other. As we contemplated God's call on our lives, we became aware that there was a great need for a spiritual awakening, so together, we launched out in an effort to help redeem the times by making life meaningful for others through a relationship with the Lord. This book tells our story.

Chapter One
Earl's Background, Birth, and Childhood

1.
Earl's Roots on His Father's Side

As the name Stuckenbruck would imply, my husband's roots on his father's side can be traced to Germany. His paternal great-grandfather, Fredrick Stuckenbruck, was born July 10, 1812, in Hesse, Darmstadt, Germany, and came to the United States with a brother (and perhaps a sister also) in the 1830s or 1840s. They settled in Ohio where he met and married Jane Baughman. The couple eventually moved to Tipton, Iowa, where they farmed some land and were blessed with five children. Their third child, George Washington, born January 16, 1855, was Earl's grandfather.

George was fifteen when his father died, and now he had to do odd jobs to help meet family expenses, which included "picking" chickens. School was held at intervals during the year when it would not interfere with the planting and harvesting of crops on the farm in the summer, or when it was not too cold in the winter. A local lawyer encouraged George's desire to become an attorney by loaning him law books to read. George even sat in on some court cases. Not able to pursue that career, however, he attended the Cedar Falls Normal School for ten weeks and earned a certificate which qualified him to teach school in a one-room schoolhouse (it is assumed grades one to eight). When, however, someone voiced a complaint, he quit.

Sometime during the 1870s, George and a friend, Marvin Goodale, responded to the challenging slogan of the day, "Go West

Young Man," and set their sights on Lake City, Iowa. This meant traveling two hundred miles on dirt roads in a wagon hitched to a team of mules as there were neither railroads nor paved roads into Lake City. Upon his arrival, George purchased forty acres of land five miles southeast of Lake City at $25 dollars an acre and then returned to his home in Tipton. Marvin took his family to their new home in 1881 but it was ten years later before George followed suit. Meanwhile, he farmed four acres near Tipton, married Laura Goodale and they had two children: Carroll Orin, named for Laura's brother, Orin, who was drowned in a swimming accident, and Clifford, who died at 18 months of pneumonia.

At first, Laura was not too eager to pioneer a new life in Lake City, but eventually chose this alternative rather than rear her children in the Tipton community which, she had discovered, included a number of "rough" families. George went ahead of his family to Lake City in the spring of 1891, and, being a carpenter of sorts, put up a shed on his forty acres in which he lived while he built a house out of lumber he had brought with him from Tipton, since there was now a railway and paved roads. Before winter set in, the new home was ready for occupancy and George went for his family.

Carroll Orin Stuckenbruck, Earl's father, was five years old when the family moved to Lake City. April 14, 1982, Eldon Waters, a resident of Lake City, wrote an article in the *Lake City Graphic* about the history of this farming community:

> Everything has a beginning and a process of growth. Today we look at Lake City's growth throughout the past 125 years. Lake City's evolution encompassed pioneer development opportunity for the good life, prosperity, and economic calamity. For example, we were once the county seat, but we lost it. We were once a 'boom-town' railroad center with executive offices and maintenance shops employing a large number of people, but like the court house, it was taken away, causing great economic shock and loss of

population. The year was 1922, and we can say that the roaring twenties struck Lake City with the force of a roaring tornado. The roaring twenties ended with the international stock market crash of 1929, followed by the great depression of the 1930s.

The first move towards the establishment of a town was made on January 7, 1856. It was the first town in Calhoun County. In 1881, there was a population of 608 or about 130 families. By the year 1900, the population had expanded to 2,703 or about 600 families. The railroad division center operated out of Lake City for approximately thirty years, and when they moved their employees from Lake City to Sioux City, the city was left with a lot of vacant homes, and with the great depression that was soon to come, property values were practically zilch. Lake City had the first Calhoun county school. Water works were introduced in 1893. An electric generating plant came in 1894.

To consummate the evolution of Lake City, we can take great pride in a humble but progressive beginning, extending into a prosperous, affluent and Christian society. When Lake City was struck by events that caused economic suppression, its citizens fought hard to overcome adversity. Lake City is one of the finest communities of its size in the state of Iowa. Let us be forever mindful that we live in the present, we build for the future—but we inherit from the past.

People today question where Lake City got its name since there is no sign of a lake in the area. Louroe, however, Carroll's sister and twelve years his junior, could remember passing by Pond Grove Lake, two miles east of Lake City, every time they drove into town when she was young. It eventually became a sort of resort area and a few cottages were built beside the lake. Later, the lake was drained and used for farm land.

Lake City could, at one time, boast of an opera house where well known groups performed. Louroe tells about a time when William Jennings Bryan came to town for a week of lectures. All the neighbors went to hear him, but she had red measles and she and her mother had to stay home. She remembers that her mother didn't like being alone out in the country.

Both Carroll and Louroe began their school days in the one-room Prairie Hall School, two miles from their home in the country. When Carroll was ready for high school, he rode horseback the five miles to school in Lake City. Eventually, he used a topless buggy hitched to his beloved horse, Bird. While at school, Carroll would tie his horse to a hitching post and sometimes, when the weather was a problem, he rented a stall in a barn. A buggy was also used to transport the family to church in Lake City. In winter, they heated stones to keep their feet warm and used robes made from cow hides for covers while traveling in the carriage.

Carroll was an avid student. He was popular, too, and in his senior year, he was selected to play the part of Shylock in Shakespeare's "Merchant of Venice." He did not enter college immediately after graduating but spent one year earning money by painting barns and putting dates on them.

When Louroe was ready for high school, the family moved into Lake City. Louroe confessed later in life that she never did graduate. She passed an exam, however, which allowed her to be accepted at a college in Des Moines to train as a nurse. In the meantime, her mother became ill and Louroe returned home to care for her. After her mother died, she remained in the home to care for her ailing father. Following his death, she returned to college, became a teacher and, for a time, was principal of a school in Lake City.

When Carroll had children, Louroe became like a sister to her nephews, Earl and Harry. She was their confidant, encourager, and helper and she continued to feel responsible for their welfare even after they became grown men. While Earl and I were overseas, we frequently received care parcels from Aunt Louroe.

Carroll eventually enrolled at Drake University in Des Moines where he did his undergraduate work. Having made the decision to become a minister, he continued his education at Drake Divinity

School. His professors were of great encouragement to him, especially Dr. Frederick D. Kershner.

During his senior year in seminary, Carroll preached his first sermon at Adaza, Iowa, in northern Green County. I found the following description of Adaza in an old newspaper. In the early 1900s, "the town grew like a child, and by the 1930s, it contained two elevators, two churches, a grade school, a bank, a creamery, a hotel, a general store, a post office, a café, a barbershop, a lumberyard, a blacksmith shop, the stockyards, and many homes. After World War II, the highway that was Adaza's main street moved outside of town and one by one the businesses closed and the buildings came down until all that remained was an elevator, and what used to be a town became a cow pasture." This is what happened to so many small communities as our country progressed.

2
Earl's Roots on His Mother's Side

Through Dorcus Collier, his great-grandmother on his mother's side, Earl could trace his roots back to the Renfro family who came from Renfrewshire, Scotland. (There are three spellings of the name: Renfrue, Renfro, and Renfrew.) King James VI of Scotland originated the name Renfrew. He gave his first son, the Prince of Wales, the title, "Baron of Renfrew." It is thought that Mark Renfro (b. 1760 – d. 1811), a distant relative of Earl's, who fought in the Revolutionary War, was a descendant of King James VI.

Earl and I were once visiting Edinburgh Castle and I told the guide about Earl having possibly been descended from James VI of Scotland. He led us around a corner of the castle tower and pointed out a rather small slab of concrete in the wall and said that behind that slab of concrete lies the real King James VI. He died in infancy, and someone went down into the slums of the city and brought up a baby who grew up to be King James VI of Scotland/

King James 1 of England! That probably was just a tale, but we found it interesting. I teased Earl afterwards, saying that he was descended from the "slums of Edinburgh!"

Dorcus was a lifelong member of the Christian Church of which her husband, Benjamin Chesnut, was a minister, and, by all accounts, an excellent preacher. Dorcus and Benjamin had a son, Granville, who married Juliana Greybeal who bore him thirteen children. The story of their lives could fill a book!

The family of Earl's grandparents on his mother's side. Granville & Juliana Chestnut. Top row, left, are Earl's parents, Carrol & May Stuckenbruck. Bottom row, right, are Earl & Harry.

Juliana was born in West Jefferson, North Carolina, June 7, 1854, and registered in Asheville. When she was four years old, she came with her parents to Kentucky on the Boone Trail, passing through Cumberland Gap. Juliana was a descendent of Daniel Boone's sister, Sarah, whose husband, John Wilcoxan, was killed by Indians during the Revolutionary War.

Juliana received her education at Laurel Seminary which was the first institution of higher learning in eastern Kentucky. She then taught school in London, Kentucky, which her husband's ancestors were said to have founded. After her marriage to Granville Chestnut, she and her husband lived with her in-laws, Benjamin and Dorcus Chestnut, at their farm in Keaney, nine miles south of London. Granville, who, by the way, was Earl's maternal grandfather, became an insurance agent and did some farming on the side. He had a roving nature and the family moved many times. They finally settled in Des Moines, Iowa, in the early winter of 1900, and called it their home for the next twenty-two years. Granville was also somewhat of an entrepreneur and homesteaded land in Torrington, Wyoming. At one time he managed West Side Hotel in Spirit Lake, Iowa.

Often away from home, Granville became a prolific letter-writer. He once wrote the following story to a friend about his grandchildren: "Talking about babies—here is a baby story that I think is hard to beat. One of my sons has two little boys about four or five and seven years old. Not long ago the younger one, who has been going to Sunday school with his older brother lately, jumped out of bed one morning and started for the cupboard. Then he stopped on the way and turned back, saying, 'Thou shalt not steal a cupcake!'"

Earl Roy remembered his Chesnut grandparents well, especially his grandmother, Juliana. Granville was gone a lot of the time, and Juliana did not always know his whereabouts. At times, food was hardly adequate, but she was patient and non-complaining. Earl recalled visiting his grandmother when his university debate team was in a competition at Drake University. He bought some groceries for her, and she prepared a delicious meal for him, her daughter Mollie, and herself. That was the last time he saw her for she died nine months after her husband on February 20, 1939. Juliana and Granville are buried in the Spirit Lake Cemetery, Iowa, along with other family members.

Earl's mother, Olivia May Chesnut, known to all and sundry as simply "May," was born December 15, 1887, to Granville and Juliana on a farm about two miles south of Woodbine, Kentucky, at what was known as Gap of the Ridge. The first racetrack in eastern Kentucky was in Woodbine, and the Christian Church which May and her family attended is still standing to this day.

Being the eighth of thirteen children, May had to help with the rearing of her younger siblings. Becoming a Christian early in life, she had a great influence on her younger brother, Lee. She motivated him and helped him achieve his goals. From an early age she took him to church with her. Her high ideals governed her life and that of Lee. Later she wrote down her goals:

> I want to have pure thoughts and pure words. I want my words to have distinct pronunciation. I will live one day at a time and not dread the things that may never happen. I will be happy because I have so much to do. I want to adjust myself to my work, and not discuss all my problems and complaints with people. I will be reserved in speech and sincere in any commendations of others. I will keep two feet on the floor. I will take time to sleep and eat breakfast. I want to smile and see the funny side of things. I want to pray longer each day. I want to keep the sacred conversations and thoughts in my own heart. I will not talk over things with the girls. I want to be calm and peaceful." (Copied from May's diary.)

May was beautiful, conscientious, and especially talented in visual arts and music. In North High School in Des Moines, she belonged to a Civics Round Table Club, a distinctively freshman organization for drill in debate and supplementary study in civil government. She sang soprano in the Glee Club, played bass drum in the high school band, and belonged to a club for junior girls for the laudable purpose of intellectual improvement. Nearly all the members were artistic and the club coffers were kept filled with profits from their own handiwork. At one time fifteen dollars were earned from the sale of valentines.

Upon graduation from high school, May enrolled in the Conservatory of Music at Drake University, majoring in piano and harmony. After receiving her degree, she taught piano and harmony at the Conservatory for two years.

May met her future husband, Carroll, at a prayer-meeting at Mondamin Christian Church in Des Moines, Iowa. Soon, they were meeting often though it was about three weeks before May was invited by Mr. Stuckenbruck to call him "Carroll." In her diary, May said again and again how much she respected him and wanted to live in such a way as to be worthy of him. One Sunday, Carroll arranged for a substitute to fill in for him at his preaching point at Rinard so that he could preach a "trial" sermon especially for May at Mondamin Christian Church. He wanted to be sure that, in the future, she would be able to enjoy hearing him preach and she remembers how proud she was of him that day.

Carroll and May became engaged and looked forward to their wedding which was extremely simple as their finances could not allow an elaborate affair. Earlier that year, Carroll's parents had moved from the country into Lake City. It was not unusual in those days for wedding ceremonies to be performed in a home, and so, on June 25, 1913, Carroll and May were married in the home of Carroll's parents with Rev. Kleckner, Carroll's friend, officiating. For a wedding gift, Carroll gave May a new Baldwin upright piano which was passed on to their son, Earl, and his family upon her death and is still an indispensable part of his daughter Jane's piano studio.

The newly-weds soon learned what it meant to economize. Carroll's father, George, bought an Overland car and let his son use it. For twelve years, it served Carroll well as he ministered to three congregations. True, it moseyed along at eighteen miles an hour, but was adequate for his needs.

Soon after their marriage, Woodlawn Christian Church in Lake City called Carroll to be their minister. Most of the locals knew the Stuckenbruck family and were proud that one of their own had become a minister. For Carroll and May, it was "coming home."

They had been married three years when their eldest son, Earl, was born. Soon afterwards, Carroll was called to minister in First Christian Church in Council Bluffs, Iowa, where he served for seven years. The church grew in leaps and bounds during his ministry and he became known as one of the leading orators among the ministers of Iowa.

It was in Council Bluffs that Harry, Carroll's second son, was born. It was also here that Earl's mother became an ordained minister. It was reasoned that she could be more helpful to her husband in the work of the church if she had the credential of an ordained minister. Often engaged couples would stop by the church to be married. If Carroll was not in the office, sometimes the couples would go to the parsonage to be married. Earl learned to write his name at an early age, and was allowed to act as witness and sign the papers of the married couples, at whose weddings his mother officiated.

A Council Bluffs paper recorded one of these events in an article titled: "Pastor's Wife Ties Matrimonial Knot." The article states:

> For just a brief period of time, it looked as though Cupid would frown upon Memorial Day marriages last Thursday afternoon when W.P. Utman of Hudson, Wis. and Margaret Coulthard of Missouri Valley called at the home of Rev. C.O. Stuckenbruck in this city to be married. Mr. Stuckenbruck was out of the city at the time and the disappointed couple were about to depart when the wife of the minister came to the rescue. Mrs. Stuckenbruck is a licensed minister and proposed that it would be a pleasure for her to perform the ceremony in the absence of her husband. The pleasure was mutual, and a pretty little marriage ceremony was soon performed which made the couple one....

In 1925, Carroll accepted a call to First Christian Church at Beatrice, Nebraska, where he served until 1931. The membership grew to over 800 and the church was able to pay off the mortgage. The list of marriages and funerals Carroll conducted is phenomenal. Many years later there came an announcement in the *Johnson City Press* in Tennessee of the 75th wedding anniversary of Robert Sandusky and the former Velda Love Hull on October 5, 2005. "The couple was married October 5, 1930, in the home of the bride in Beatrice, NE, with Rev. Stuckenbruck officiating," the paper stated.

May was a member of various societies. In 1941, she served as vice president of the International Convention of Disciples of Christ which met in St. Louis, MO. On the evening she presided, Champ Clark, a prominent American Democrat, and Charles A. Lindbergh, author of *Transatlantic Flight that Shook the World*, were speaking against war in a large arena nearby (seating capacity 16,000) at Forest Park. Faced with a dilemma, her husband went to hear them instead of his wife!

While in Nebraska, May spent a lot of time tracing her roots and those of Carroll. Genealogy became a passion for her. She discovered that she was a Daughter of the American Revolution through five different lines: George W. Jewett, president of The Jewett Family of America, once wrote May: "I note that you are descended from Humphrey de Bohun. Yes, that makes us related and that carries you back to nearly every king of Europe, even back to some of the Caesars of Rome and back to Abraham, Isaac and Jacob and Ruth....Yes, you are about 100 generations from David and Soloman, your ancestors. So you see, you have some good ones to offset William the Conqueror."

Years later, when May's grandson Loren was a fourth grade student at Cherokee Elementary School in Johnson City, Tennessee, his teacher was amazed when he announced that his family was descended from Adam and demanded evidence. For proof, he copied his grandmother's lineage back to Adam to show his teacher. She probably remained somewhat skeptical but at least she knew where he was coming from.

Carroll and May became aware that they needed to seek out a locality which would provide a very good school system for their boys, and so Carroll accepted a call as minister of Hillside Christian Church in Wichita, Kansas. The Stuckenbrucks had been with the church in Beatrice for six years. Their "farewell reception was most impressive," an article in the local paper stated: "It bore witness of the regret which Beatrice feels at the departure of this estimable family." Mrs. Stuckenbruck was presented with a tooled leather purse and Rev. Stuckenbruck with a leather traveling bag. Sadly, a year after they left Beatrice and a week before a succeeding minister was to arrive, the church burned. However, it was soon rebuilt.

In March, 1931, Carroll began his ministry in Hillside Christian Church in Wichita. His previous experience made him well able to recognize the needs and opportunities of a young and rapidly growing congregation. The church had been started in 1922, and Carroll was only the second pastor. The women of the congregation were very active and made a number of outstanding contributions to every phase of the church life during the years of Carroll's ministry. The pipe organ, grand piano, kitchen equipment, elevator, and library were concrete evidence of their endeavors. In February, 1931, the women even bought the church parsonage!

On May 17, 1939, everyone gathered to burn the church mortgage. This brought back memories of preceding years when what became known as the famous Hillside "jitney dinners" had provided a large amount of funds to help pay off the debt. Church members had thought of several ways to raise money and came up with the idea of organizing weekly church dinners when those present were charged five cents for each item chosen from the menu. The sum accumulated was amazing and greatly helped towards paying off the debt.

Carrol once wrote, "We are followers of Christ, not because we know all about Him, but because what we do know causes us to trust Him beyond our knowledge."

3
Earl's Birth and Childhood

As previously mentioned, Earl was born three years after Carroll and May were married. On October 30, 1916, he was delivered at home by the family physician, Dr. McVey. His parents named him Earl Roy, but he was known to family and friends simply as Earl. It was a blessed time for the parents, as the church family, relatives, and friends were able to share their joy. May's mother, of course, was overjoyed and wrote:

> My dear Carroll and May and precious little baby,
> We are glad you are all getting along so well. It was good of Louroe to write to us for you. I know she was disappointed that the baby was not a girl, but she'll love it just the same. Such soft, silky, pretty hair it has and such a pretty name too. Would like so much to see the little darling, but after your description I can almost imagine how pretty and sweet he is. Hope you both continue to get along. . . .Am so thankful you have such good care and help and hope you will feel real well and strong soon.
> With much love, Mama.

Shortly after Carroll and May moved to Council Bluffs and exactly one year minus two days after the birth of their first child, a second son, Harry Lee, was born. The two brothers grew up almost like twins, sharing the same interests and participating in the same activities all the way through middle school. Earl remembers that the school in Council Bluffs was a multi-story building with a chute on each floor for students to use in case of fire.

Once, the C.B. Sousa Band came to town and Earl was impressed when he heard the band perform and was inspired to eventually take up the trombone.

Family vacations were usually spent with the Stuckenbruck grandparents in Lake City or the Chesnut grandparents in Des Moines. Grandparents George and Laura Stuckenbruck's home in Lake City was located at the corner of Main and Lincoln streets. George kept scraps of boards and tools in a shed so that the boys could make things when they came to visit. Some of the items they made were kept and used in their own homes in later years. I can recall seeing various things they had created—book holders made out of wood and shoe polish boxes which came in handy when, every Saturday evening, all the family shoes were polished in preparation for the "Sabbath."

May was often the speaker at various programs and she would take her sons along to provide special music. She taught them to play rhythms on a broom-stick and with spoons and other "instruments." Earl learned to play the violin and May would accompany the boys on the piano. Once, when Earl heard some visiting musicians, Charlie and Maude Howe, playing music on goblets and the saw, he was very impressed and so Mr. Howe bought a set of goblets for him and taught him and his brother how to play the musical saw.

While the family was in Beatrice, Earl suffered from rheumatic fever in 1928, at age twelve, and missed a year of school. It happened to be the year Hoover and Al Smith were running for president and, while in bed, Earl would listen to their speeches on the radio. Because he had to miss a year in school, he and Harry were in the same class from then on.

The principal of the high school in Wichita which Earl attended recognized his potential and suggested books for him to read and discussed them with him. He and Harry excelled academically and socially.

Earl learned to play the trombone and Harry played the clarinet. They marched in the band. Earl wrote his Stuckenbruck grandparents that things were going well. "This afternoon (Nov.

18, 1934) Harry and I have been playing in an orchestra called the Wichita Symphony Orchestra. We are not in the class with those outstanding symphonies in the East despite the fact that the names are similar. It is composed of high school musicians and would-be professionals, and we give a concert every month....For me, mathematics is over. I have finished with Algebra and Trigonometry. I rather enjoy playing with figures."

Lucile Ford, missionary to Kulpaharth, India, once wrote: "Earl, I can truly say that yours is the most ideal home I have ever known. You had music, books, work, play, and fun, good food and nice clothing, toys–even dolls and doll buggies. You see, I know because I have your pictures. I have many in my album of you and Harry and always enjoy looking at them. I could not wish for better friends than your parents have been to me all these many years."

4
Earl's Teenage and College Years

In 1940, Carroll accepted the pastorate of First Christian Church in Topeka, Kansas. Here, Earl was awarded the coveted Summerfield scholarship to attend Kansas University. It covered his tuition, room and board, and books! The only thing it didn't cover was postage to send his laundry home to be done. Harry, meanwhile, had become interested in "homing pigeons" and, in order to care for them, he remained for a year as a student at a business college in Topeka before joining Earl at K.U.

Both Earl and Harry were in the K.U. band. Harry was treasurer some of the time. The band, of course, played for all the ball games. The story is told of the band accompanying the team to Washington, D.C. At a rest stop, Earl and a friend were left behind. They had to summon a taxi to catch up with the bus that carried the band. The team had not missed them!

Earl was an outstanding debater in high school and during his first year in college. However, after debating that first year at K.U. with a winning team, he decided that "one cannot debate the truth," and gave it up.

While at K.U., Harry had to have an appendectomy. Earl was allowed to observe the surgery. However, during preparation time, he became faint and had to be led from the room. The only phone call he made to his parents during his college days at K.U. was about Harry's illness.

Earl will never forget the near escape he had while at K.U. Sledding down a hill one winter, he came to a wire fence and had he not ducked his head to slide under it, it would have been severed from his body. Those watching breathed a sigh of relief when they saw that he was safe.

Earl and Harry spent their summer vacations while in college at Cheeley Camp in Colorado as counselors and recreation leaders for boys. The fresh air and experiences in the mountains helped refresh them for their winters at the university.

During the school year, Earl took Bible classes on campus at K.U. from Harold Barr, chairman of the Bible Department, and preached his first sermon during his senior year at the North Christian Church in Lawrence at the invitation of the minister, Leonard Wymore. Leonard's wife, Thelma Hoss Wymore, who served as director of the North American Christian Convention for twenty-four years, remembered hearing Earl preach his first sermon, but neither he nor she could recall his subject.

He was elected to Phi Beta Kappa, Psi Chi, and to Sachem, "a distinction given to men who were making progress in their particular field of endeavor, who were leading in student affairs, and who had made valuable contributions to the university." He was frequently invited to play special music on his saw with someone accompanying him on the piano for programs both on campus and in the community.

Earl, May, Carrol & Harry Stuckenbruck.

In 1939, Earl and Harry graduated from Kansas University—Harry with a business major and Earl with a double major: one in psychology and the other in philosophy. He decided to enter the ministry. His father's friend, Frederick D. Kershner, had left Des Moines and was now dean of The School of Religion at Butler University in Indianapolis, Indiana. On the advice of his father, Earl enrolled in that seminary, while Harry accepted a position with the Massachusetts Mutual Life Insurance Company in Springfield, Mass.

Chapter Two
Ottie Mearl's Background, Birth, and Childhood

1.
Ottie Mearl's Roots On Her Father's Side

Peggy Henderson in her book, *Memoirs of Randolph, Bibb County, Alabama*, describes how pioneers first settled the area in which I was born:

> Many hundreds of people flowed through Alabama, and Bibb County during the early 1800's looking for a better life. Many also stayed in our area [the Talladega National Forest] for a time and then traveled onward searching for their dream. But many also stayed permanently. These were the pioneers who, not only cleared the land, built houses and barns, they did much more. They brought with them their 'American Dream.' They brought their morals and values. They brought their faith in God. They brought their talents and work ethic. They brought their sense of civic duty and community. They built churches and schools. They brought leadership and a sense of responsibility for developing a structure of government in which freedom, justice and order prevailed. These first pioneers had a huge and very difficult job. Every generation since has progressed, but no other generation since has lived through the trials and struggles of the first pioneers. We owe them our gratitude and respect."—Used by permission.

Some of those pioneers were my ancestors whose descendants founded Randolph, the largest community in the county, because it had a railroad, built around 1852, which served passengers as well as freight. And so, when forests were cleared to make room for houses and farms, the lumber could be loaded onto trains at Randolph. It was also a convenient way to both ship out cotton and corn, the two main crops in the area, as well as receive food and supplies.

My grandfather's family with my father, Orton, on the left.

Understandably, industries also sprang up as a result of the railway. The first settlers in the Tabernacle, Lawley, and Randolph communities were involved in the forest industry. They cut crossties for railroad tracks and sold them for twenty-five cents each. The ties were hauled to Randolph on wagons, pulled by oxen, and shipped out on the M&O Railroad. Before the railroad came through Randolph, the nearest trading post was Selma, fifty miles away. People would go there in wagons pulled by oxen to load up with food they did not grow themselves as well as other supplies for the year. Sometimes they would be gone for several weeks.

During those early days, it was not easy for the settlers to buy clothes for their growing children. They would "seed" and "card" cotton and spin it into thread on their spinning wheels which was then used to make cloth that they dyed with birch bark. I can remember helping to "seed" cotton and then to "card" it for use as a "filler" for quilts.

Open range allowed cattle and other animals to roam at will. People trapped and killed them for meat. There were hog killings when the weather was cold enough in the fall and neighbors would come together for the event. Several hogs were killed at the same time and the meat divided. Then it would be preserved by hanging it in smokehouses where it was salted and smoked. If their meat gave out before the next butchering time, the women would scratch up salt from the earth in the smoke houses, boil it, and use the salted water for cooking. They did not have stoves for cooking and used fire places instead, which sometimes covered half a wall. During cold weather, people would sometimes heat large stones by the fireplace and use them for warmth while sleeping. They slept on homemade beds, the bottom part of which was constructed of corded ropes. The mattresses were made of hay and enclosed in ticking. The covers were made from feathers picked from geese and enclosed in fabric. All this and more comprised the life of my pioneer ancestors in Alabama.

My paternal great-grandparents on my father's side, William and Olive Lawrence, were among these pioneers who settled in

Maplesville, not far from Randolph. William enlisted in the Confederate Army during the Civil War, was wounded in Wilderness, VA, and then discharged due to disability. An extract from his obituary, written by an uncle, Walt Edwards, reads as follows:

> William S. Lawrence was born Oct. 13, 1830 and died June 23, 1893. He joined the Methodist Church in early manhood in which he lived a consistent member to the day he died. He was living with his second wife and was the father of seven children, six of whom are living. For a long time he had suffered unknown pain, being afflicted with dropsy. Like Job, with patience he endured to the end. For several years he had been making preparation to welcome death, and thus on Friday night, June 23, when He, who doeth all things well, saw fit to remove him from earth to his reward. All during his sickness he would talk of the Church, and its institution. He was Sunday School Superintendent, for he believed in Sunday school. He was a class leader for he loved to inquire into the spiritual condition of the Church. He was Steward for he loved to support the Gospel. He was everything he could be for the building up of Christ's Kingdom here on earth. But he has gone to that building not made with hands, Eternal in the Heavens. We mourn our loss. It is his gain. He leaves many loved ones here. One more vacant seat on earth, one more occupied around the Throne of God in heaven. He is now singing the sweet songs of Angels. For he often said he could not sing here, but he would sing when he got home. Our home is darkened by the loss of a father, but many bright rays of light shine in our pathway as we journey through this world of woe. We should take warning and heed the many exhortations and be led by the prayers of one who was dear to us, to follow in his footprints and by and by we will meet again, where parting is no more—where congregations ne'er break up and Sabbaths never end.

William married Olive Ann, born Jan. 17, 1841, and died August 8, 1870. They are both buried in Maplesville in the cemetery of Old Pleasant Hill Methodist Church where they were members. The church is no longer standing.

William and Olive's son, Jasper Branson Bryant Lawrence ("Pap," as he was lovingly called by his grandchildren), was my paternal grandfather and was born April 26, 1867, and died April 24, 1935. He married my grandmother, Agnes Ella Estella Edwards, who was born April 29, 1866, and died December 18, 1917. My father, Orton Spinx, was one of their seven children and was born in the Lawley community.

William Stanford Edwards, my paternal great-grandfather on my grandmother's side, was born December 13, 1818, in Randolph, N.C. and died July 2, 1882, in Bibb County, Alabama. He and his wife, Martha Jane Morgan, migrated from Randolph County, N.C., via Uniontown, Alabama, to Bibb County in 1830. They arrived in a covered wagon and homesteaded the land around Tabernacle where a church and a school were later built. During the Civil War (1861–1865), my great-grandfather, his son, and son-in-law walked from Bibb County to Gettysburg, PA, and fought in the Battle of Gettysburg. While they were gone, Wilson's raiders came through Bibb County. They destroyed the Tabernacle Methodist Church building. William's wife, Martha, and daughter, Lou Quincy, were working in their garden to raise food for the family. The raiders took their gardening tools and fled.

Both of my paternal great-grandfathers were, according to Carol Lawrence Vidale's research, "lay preachers." Both were stewards and very active in the Methodist churches of which they were members. In fact, William S. Edwards was instrumental in helping to start Tabernacle Episcopal Methodist Church while his wife, Martha, began the first Sunday school there in Bibb County. Rules for membership were rather strict. History records that one woman was expelled from membership because she gave birth to an Indian baby, while another suffered the same fate for playing cards on Sunday. A few black people sometimes attended and sat in the back of the church.

My relatives have been members of Tabernacle Episcopal Methodist Church down through the years, and family reunions continue to be held there. This is not surprising as the names of my grandparents are on the first official members' roster of the church.

2.
Ottie Mearl's Roots On Her Mother's Side

Louis and Sarah Henderson Wallace were my maternal great-grandparents. Louis was an immigrant from Ireland and worked on a ship to earn his passage to America. He obtained a land grant in Alabama where he settled with his wife, Sarah Jane, who was one of nine children. Her father, Franklin Henderson, served in the Confederate Army during the Civil War. His signature was spoken of as "his mark" as he could neither read nor write.

Louis is reputed to have had a liking for cheese and so friends and family tried to keep him well supplied. In addition to farming, he was a tanner of leather which he sold for shoe strings, horse harnesses, and chair bottoms and backs. Elton, my brother, and our father, Orton S. Lawrence, visited Louis' old homestead place which was located in a beautiful valley in Alabama. They ate pears from a tree in the yard that Louis had planted and drank water from the spring that had served him and his family.

Sarah and Louis had four children. The eldest, James Monroe, was my grandfather. He was born September 27, 1876, and died November 18, 1952. He married Dovie Miranda Harris October 11, 1896, at Bethlehem, Alabama. Grandmother was of Indian and Dutch descent, I am told, and came to the United States from some island. Regrettably, I have no further information which would help explain Dovie's lineage.

My grandparents, Monroe and Dovie, ran a dairy. For many years, family reunions were held in their home. They were very devout Christians. My two sisters, Peacie and Gertha, and I spent one summer vacation with them and I recall my grandmother, in her long white gown, kneeling by her bed in the evenings. She would pray aloud, and we always listened for we knew she was sure to mention our names.

Monroe and Dovie had thirteen children including two sets of twins. One of their children, Lester, gave money to build a Nazarene church in his parents' honor in Vance, Alabama, where they lived. It was called Wallace Chapel.

My brother Elton tells a story about a summer vacation he spent with our Wallace grandparents when he was about twelve years old. Transportation was hard to come by, and so our father drew a map for him to find his way on foot to their home. Armed with his backpack and directions, he set out around four o'clock one morning and walked several miles before a truck driver gave him a ride to an uncle's house. His uncle knew the truck-driver and paid him to take Buddy, as he was called, on to his destination. He was received with open arms by our grandparents and thoroughly spoiled, an experience he would never forget.

3.
Birth and Childhood of Ottie Mearl

Growing up in Alabama in the 1920s and 30s, I was totally unaware that everything I was learning and experiencing was preparing me to enter missionary service, and that Earl and I would journey together into a pioneering ministry abroad for the Lord. God knew, however, and, looking back, I can see His hand in even the smallest circumstances.

There were three, closely-knit communities in Alabama where I grew up: Tabernacle, Lawley, and Randolph. Tabernacle had a church, a school and at one time, a grist mill. Some say there was a hat shop as well. Lawley had a post office, store, and school. In Randolph, there was a thirty-three-room, three story hotel which served as the social center of the community. It also accommodated locals and guests. (Two of my sisters, Gertha and Peacie, remember seeing the hotel on fire, Sunday, February 13, 1944, as they arrived home by train from Selma where they were employed. It was never rebuilt.) In addition, there were two churches, a post office, a train depot, a cotton gin, an academy, a school, a mattress factory, a ladies' hat shop, a few other stores, and a bowling alley. Now, in 2015, there are only a gas station, a convenience store, a church, a post office and, more recently, a restaurant in Randolph.

Our family lived in a house down the hill behind Tabernacle Church. My parents, Orton Spinx, and my mother, Rena Ardelle Wallace Lawrence, were married September 29, 1918 in the Cox community by a probate judge, W.J. Nicholson. They already had a three–year–old son, Elton Marlton, known by us all as "Buddy," by the time they were expecting me. Buddy once related to me the following story:

Any day my parents were expecting their second child. The midwife, a distant cousin named Ms. Chism, was alerted that the time for my birth had come. Buddy was playing with chickens in the yard when she arrived. The chickens didn't think that was fun, and so a rooster jumped on him, flogging him. The midwife had already asked Buddy to leave the chickens alone and to come inside but he had not heeded her. Now she was in a dilemma. She was in the midst of the delivery, and she didn't know whether to save him or me! I have to give Buddy credit for being a good storyteller. He could have entertained an audience at one of the International Storytelling Festivals in Jonesborough, Tennessee!

All went well, however, and my birth certificate states that a Dr. J.S. Cleveland certified that he "attended the birth of this child, Ottie Mearl Lawrence, born alive at 11 a.m., April 29, 1922, at Lawley, Bibb County, Alabama." His wife signed the certificate as a witness.

It was my mother who chose my name. She found the two names, Ottie and Mearl, in two separate magazine articles, I am told. A person who attaches a name to a newborn cannot always be sure it will suit his or her personality. Sometimes people even want to change their names. My name is unique, however, and I like that about it, although I do not like to be called "Ottie" alone.

It is so flat-sounding—no music there. I can tolerate being called "Mearl" alone, but I prefer being called by both names—Ottie Mearl, or better yet, spell the two names together—Ottiemearl. Is it a coincident that my soul mate's name is "Earl" which rhymes with "Mearl"? If, for some reason, I would be asked to select another name for myself, I would choose "Phoebe—a helper," remembering Romans 16:1.

My father, mother & four siblings.

The story is told that one day while we were living in the house down the hill from the Tabernacle Church, Buddy was sitting by a window, looking out. Mother was milking our cow, Daisy, in the barn. Now Daisy had long horns and jammed them into some timber and in the process, had somehow or other, pinned Mother down so that she could not get away. Since she was gone so long, Buddy went looking for her. When he saw what was happening, he said, "I'll help you, Mother." He picked up a 4 x 4. It was heavy and he let it fall. The frightened cow dislodged its horns from the timber and Mother was freed. Daddy was out laying crossties for a railroad track. When he came home, he cut off the cow's horns and packed the stubs with tar.

When Buddy was three, he ran away from home. He said he held onto his dog's tail to help him climb up the hill toward Tabernacle Methodist Episcopal Church. Mother knew if she could find the dog she would find Buddy. She called and the dog barked. At the top of the hill she found them at Aunt Analyzer's house. Aunt Analyzer was my great aunt, my grandmother's sister, and it was planned that, if Mother was cross because Buddy had run away, she would hide him until she cooled down.

I am told that Mother was very quiet and religious and kept a clean house. Every evening after we had had our baths, she would read to us and she taught us to pray a prayer that went something like this:

> "Dear Father:
> Help me to do whatever is right
> Make it then my chief delight
> To love Thee while I live."

Tears welled up in Buddy's eyes when he told me years later that he had often repeated that simple prayer while employed in law enforcement and also during World War II while serving overseas.

During the course of my childhood, I attended schools in all three communities: Tabernacle, Lawley, and Randolph. I recall having to walk quite a distance to the Tabernacle school on a cold morning, arriving with hands so cold that they ached. The teacher was kind and tried every way she could to warm them.

At the Lawley School, one could tell who the poor children were, for they had corn bread for their lunches instead of "light" bread. Willyne Gentry was my best friend, and I didn't want her to know that I had corn bread in my lunch pail so I pretended not to be hungry at lunch time.

Mrs. Hudson (Claudia) Williams was my teacher at the Randolph school. I adored her. Her handwriting was beautiful and I wanted my script to look like hers. Her husband taught at the school as well and had devotions every morning after we all assembled. Sometimes he was moved to tears during his devotions. Occasionally, Peacie, Gertha, and I were invited to sing during the general assemblies on Fridays. I corresponded with Mrs. Williams after I left home until I finished college and married. When I told her that Earl and I were planning our wedding, she sent five dollars and requested that we have a picture made of us together for her.

Our house was located about halfway between Centreville and Maplesville. At a young age, I remember going with my father to Centreville in a wagon drawn by a team of mules. My brother, Elton, and I would each hold onto a wooden pole. On the ends were attached padded devices which we held against the front wheels of the wagon to act as brakes while going downhill. This expedition to Centreville would take us a whole day, even though it was only a round trip of about twenty-four miles!

We moved, for a while, to Parkwood, Alabama, where Daddy worked on the railroad. We were living there when Peacie Marinder was born February 14, 1924. Peacie was a bright child and learning was easy for her. Unfortunately, her life was cut short when, on May 20, 1965, she and her six children were on their way to church on a Sunday evening and had a head-on collision with another car. Two of her children, Orton Phillip and Rhonda Gail, were also killed. Oscar, Peacie's husband, worked on the railroad and was away from home when the accident happened. It was a very traumatic time for the entire family and community. The news reached us while we were overseas. Earl

Lee, our oldest son, answered the phone when my sister, Inell, called from the home of Geneva, a cousin living in Selma, where the survivors, Monroe David, Charlie Mike, Oscar Sidney, and Pattie Grace were hospitalized, and relayed the news. He was a natural diplomat and broke the news appropriately. I could not go to my family back home. I could only weep for the loss of my sister and her children and trust God to comfort our hurting family, neighbors, and friends.

Daddy decided that he could improve the family income if we spent winters in Wauchula, Florida, picking strawberries, and summers in Lawley, Alabama, picking cotton. Gertha Louvene was added to the family January 4, 1926, while we were in Wauchula. She was a sweet, happy child. She married Glynn Scott and they had two children, Sherry Denice and Roger Glynn. They lived in the Randolph, Alabama, community all of their lives and she was "central hostess" for family members who lived away and the source for much of our family historical information.

In 1927, while we were staying in Wauchula, we were invited by Uncle Walker, Daddy's brother, and his wife, Aunt Dessie Lawrence, to live with them in Quincy Florida. Their house was out in the country. Daddy, they suggested, could help Uncle Walker cut timber for crossties for a railroad track. It was a well-paying temporary job, and Daddy consented.

Our family of six piled into our Model T Ford with as much of our earthly goods as possible and started on the trip. Mother was sitting in the front passenger seat. She was half asleep when she suggested to Daddy that we have a "rest stop" for the children. Daddy was slowing down while going down grade when Mother opened the car door before he came to a halt and fell out onto the pavement. Daddy tried to catch her, but failed. He stopped the car, ran back, and picked her up in his arms. She was bleeding on the head. He took her to a hospital in Bartow where she stayed until she was well enough for us to complete our journey. She was with child at the time and never fully recovered from the accident.

The house where we lived in Quincy was quite primitive. It was set up on huge stone blocks and at night we could hear sheep bumping around underneath. Buddy, as usual, had many adventures. One day he left his sweater at school and had to go back and get it. On the way, he had to pass houses in a pasture where some black people lived. He told a little boy that he would give him a whistle he had made if he would go with him. It was dark when they returned to the little boy's house so Buddy asked him to go at least half way home with him. Daddy was waiting at the first gate where dangerous animals sometimes wandered. As the boys came close, Daddy made a noise like a car. That almost frightened Buddy to death, and even though Daddy called to him in order to identify himself, he ran so fast he could not stop until he reached home.

Our cousin, Elmo, Uncle Walker and Aunt Dessie's young son, became ill and died. They took him to Lawley, Alabama, and buried him in the Tabernacle cemetery. Not long after Elmo's death, Mother gave birth to a stillborn baby boy. It was later discovered that the midwife was disqualified. Mother knew that she was going to die and so she called us in, one by one, to say good-bye. She told us to be good and mind Daddy and others who would care for us. The angels, she said, assured her that we would be all right. She hugged and kissed us and told us that she loved us. Daddy and Uncle Walker made a coffin for my little baby brother and buried him under an old oak tree at the edge of Quincy, Florida. We got on a train and took Mother to Lawley, Alabama, where she was buried in the family cemetery at Tabernacle Church. I was five years old.

Uncle Walker and Aunt Dessie eventually moved back to Lawley. Uncle Walker became Sunday school superintendent at Tabernacle Episcopal Methodist Church. It was Easter Sunday afternoon in 1932 and he was on the porch of their home. He had drawn up a bucket of water from the well and was just about to drink from the dipper in his hand when a tornado swept through the area. Uncle Walker and two of their children, Ella Katherine and Austin, were killed instantly. His daughter, Dessie Lou, was stripped of her clothing and was found standing near the door of a neighbor's storm pit. She and Aunt Dessie had survived!

After Mother's death, Daddy was faced with a dilemma. He had to decide how to take care of his children. There seemed to be no other way than to stay with relatives. Aunt Nora, Mother's sister, and her husband, Uncle Jessie Campbell, invited us to live with them. They were very kind and helpful. They lived out in the country on a farm. We were there at harvest time and two black men were helping. We all sat down at a table in the dining room for meals, but food was taken out to the helpers who ate while sitting on the steps leading into the house.

Then Daddy's sister and her husband, Aunt Pansy and Uncle Simp Cox, invited us to stay with them in Bessemer. While there, I came down with double pneumonia. I remember that I could not find a cool place on the bed to lay my head. Daddy called in a doctor who was old and not much help. When the three people present—Aunt Pansy, Aunt Sadie, and a black lady who worked in the home—realized that I was not being helped by him, they took over. They put onion, garlic, mustard (and I don't know what else) on a poultice and wrapped it around my chest to keep it warm. The elderly doctor said they were doing the right thing. I was very weak while recovering and it was some time before I was able to walk alone.

While living with Aunt Pansy and Uncle Simp Cox, a flu epidemic raged in the neighborhood and they warned their children to try to avoid catching the flu. One day, their three or four-year-old son, G.S., was playing next door. They heard a cry for help: "Come quick! The ole flu has caught me!!" he was shouting. They found him hanging on a post by the galluses of his overalls. Years later, G.S. became an engineer and was stationed in Stuttgart, Germany. Learning that we were living in Tübingen, just thirty miles south of Stuttgart, he and his wife, Wini, came for a visit, bringing with them T-bone steaks!

Aunt Drudie, another of Daddy's sisters, and Uncle Walton Moore invited us to stay with them. They took us to church at Tabernacle where they were active members. Aunt Drudie was in charge of a Mother's Day program at the church and taught Buddy and me poems so that we could participate. It is assumed that she composed the poetry herself. Here is Buddy's poem:

> I was born in ole Alabama –
>   The state I love so dear.
> 'Twas there I spent my childhood days
>   With Mother ever near.
>
> 'Twas there we lived so happily
>   With playmates and my toys,
> With Mother ever near
>   Sharing my griefs and joys.
>
> There were others in our family
>   Who always gave us cheer,
> But Mother brought us sunshine
>   And drove away our fear.
>
> Then one day darkness came.
>   It drove away the sunshine
> And took our Mother away.

Aunt Drudie also taught me the following poem to recite:

> I have no mother for she died
>   When I was very young.
> But the memory still around my heart
>   Like a morning mist has hung.
>
> They tell me of an angel band
>   That watched me while I slept
> And of a soft and gentle hand
>   That wiped the tears I wept.

> That same hand held my own
> When I began to walk.
> And joy sparkled in her eyes
> When I first tried to talk.
>
> Now they say mothers' hearts are glad
> When infant charms expand.
> I wonder if she thinks of me
> In that bright and happy land.
>
> For I know she's in heaven now
> That holy place of rest,
> For she was always good to me
> And the "gooder" on her blessed.

My father finally came to the conclusion that he could not continue to live with relatives in order for them to help care for his children, and so he spoke with both a priest and a minister about his situation. Then he decided to inquire about placing us in a Catholic orphanage in Selma, Alabama, but was not very happy with the stipulation that we would have to remain there until age twelve. On the day that we were to go, Daddy received word that there was some kind of epidemic at the home and we would have to wait. He took that as a sign that God was not pleased with the idea.

About that time, Daddy began courting a young lady in the community, Ida Mae Henderson, who was our distant relative. Ida Mae and my birth mother had the same great-grandparents. Daddy and Ida Mae were married December 9, 1928, and we moved into our own home as a family in Jemison, Alabama. Daddy had to work hard to get Buddy to accept our new mother. "Mama," we called her now, was patient and kind. I'm sure the responsibility of helping to raise all of us must have been a heavy burden for her to bear. Daddy had a job working in the coal mines in Aldrich and life was not easy. The following is a letter he wrote to Mama January 15, 1930, just over a year after their marriage:

Dear little Sweetheart,

Here I come for a short chat with you. I have just finished supper and am feeling good. Truly hope these few lines will find you and all the babies O.K. Kiss them for me.

Well, I got here with as much money as I left home with. I guess Elton told you about my missing the train. I walked on to Ashby, caught a ride to Wilton and walked from there. Was somewhat tired when I got here.

Listen, I have some bad news to tell you. Straven Mines blew up yesterday evening—killed six men. Crippled two more. That place is only 5 miles from here. One of Mr. Pains' nephews was killed. Will be buried at Randolph tomorrow. I guess they will all go. Somehow, I felt sad that morning when I started down into the mines. Then when we started out, there was a Negro hurt. He was put on a stretcher and rode in the car just ahead of me. Then I went to the Post Office and heard the other news, so I saw the reason I felt bad.

Well, I am in a hurry. Write me as soon as you get this. Tell me all the news. I am still trying to get us a place. Wrote two more letters this week. Maybe we will succeed on one. Good night, Darling, and little children. Hope you all good luck until I see you again.

The same old boy, O.S. Lawrence

I started to school in Jemison. It was hard to know how to respond to still another new experience. Upon arrival at school, I laid my head down on my desk and refused to lift it until it was time to go home. This created quite a dilemma for the teacher, the class, and my family. After a couple of days and a lot of coaxing from the teacher and Daddy, I finally agreed to be a part of the class.

Christmas came. We were in a new community and acquainted with very few people. What was more, there were no funds for presents, although Daddy managed to buy a box of shredded coconut, which was a favorite with us. So, Christmas morning, he called us, one by one, into the kitchen and gave each a spoonful of coconut. He told us that he loved us. That was our Christmas present and we were content.

A year later, Jasper Bryant, named after our grandfather Lawrence and known as J.B. for short, was added to our family on October 22nd, 1929. He was born at home and I remember the joy of having a baby in the house once more. Buddy was especially glad to have another boy in the family. While still a young man, J.B. lost a hand in an accident. In spite of his handicap, he became a much sought-after piano tuner technician in the Atlanta area where he lived with his wife, Betty, and their three children: Gary Jerome, Gregory Keith, and Sheila Diane.

Just over two years after J.B.'s birth, a little sister, Eleanor Inell, was born on December 7, 1931. By this time, we had moved once more to a house near Daddy's oldest brother, Uncle Willie and his wife, Aunt Zoe, in the Lawley community. We all thought our new baby was so cute and smart. I remember, once, that she was out in the yard digging in the dirt with a spoon. I asked her what she was doing and she said, "I'm digging a hole to get to China." When she grew up, she married Emmitt Cochran and they had four children: Amy Dawn, Timothy Ray, Sandra Louise, and Donald Michael.

It was while we lived in this house that Daddy had a problem with my constant singing. It became, I suppose, somewhat annoying, for I wouldn't stop, or so I am told. Also, there must have been concern that I would awaken my baby sister, Inell. One evening Daddy decided to try a method to get me to stop. He sent me outside with instructions to stand on a stump in the yard and sing to my heart's content. I sang "When the Roll is Called up Yonder, I'll be There." Afraid of the dark, I was allowed to return inside.

I also recall that while we lived there, Mama made soap out of white ashes from the fireplace. She also found white clay and whitewashed the area around the fireplace with it.

It must have been about this time when Buddy and I attended a one-room school in the Lawley community. Miss Daisy was the teacher, and we all loved her. In preparation for school, Mama made a couple of dresses for me and bought for me a pair of shoes. When visitors would come, I was delighted to show them my dresses and shoes. It was real special to have a new pair of shoes, especially when I had been loaned a pair from my Aunt Irene every time I went to church.

In the summertime, we children helped to chop and pick cotton along with the adults. It was hard work. To encourage us, Daddy would say, "To the other end (of the row), back and then…." We hoped that "and then" meant we could quit for the day, but that was seldom the case. We were paid thirty-five cents for a hundred pounds of cotton we picked for Mr. "Lum" Tucker. The cotton was weighed every time our sacks were full.

As I picked cotton, I dreamed about what I could buy with the money I earned. We had a Sears Roebuck catalog and I leafed through it daily, looking for cloth which could be made into dresses. Of course I couldn't sew, but Mama could. To add a finishing touch to the dresses, I took scraps from some material Mama ordered for dresses and made fingerless gloves to match the dresses. Some people were impressed by the novelty, and the idea became a fad with some of our friends.

Our amusements were simple in those days. I remember when someone bought a radio, the first one in the community. We young people would gather together in the evening and listen to it. Often we would have a "peanut parching" party at the same time. The Centreville Press reported that on April 15, 1937, "Mr. Glenn Scott, Mr. Willard Henderson, Misses Inez Scott, Ottie Mearl, Peacie, and Gertha Lawrence visited Mr. and Mrs. Justice Waldrop Saturday night and listened to the radio." Another family had a Victrola on which they could play records, and this, too, was entertainment for the neighborhood children. Still another form of entertainment was telling ghost stories. Many sleepless nights followed such a session. Finally, Daddy had a little talk with us. He assured us that if anyone or anything tried to harm us in any way, they would have to deal with him first. He would take care of us. He calmed our fears and we felt secure.

On summer evenings, young people in the community would congregate on porches and sing while those who were able picked their guitars. Songs which told stories like "Barbara Allen," "Little Mary Phagan," and others were our favorites. Gospel music was also a part of our repertoire. Recently, I was able to find the story of Mary Phagan online, even the entire text of the song about her. It was a true story and had taken place in 1915!

An event, similar to the happenings in the story, took place in the Randolph community. August 8, 1921, Annie Lee Wallace, 15, was walking home from Singing School when she was killed by Clyde Thomas, a thirty-three-year-old black man who was liked by both the white and black people in the community. There was great rage when it was determined that he was the perpetrator of the crime. He was hanged in the county jail at Centreville. As far as I know, the story was never told in song, as was the story of Mary Phagan; but it was, nevertheless, passed down through generations.

Then there were the singing schools. In the summer time, Hudson Williams and his brother held these schools at Tabernacle Methodist Church, using the Stamps Baxter shaped notes songbooks. We children loved to sing and so, in exchange for sorghum syrup for pay, we were able to become a part of that experience. We were taught to read music with shaped notes and how to direct music. In addition to learning the notes, we learned the "feeling" of each note. Now, I can only remember that "mi", representing the third note of a diatonic scale, is "sad and weeping"; and "sol", a syllable representing the fifth tone in a diatonic scale, is "bright and joyous." Buddy, Branson Lawrence, Mary Ella Moore, and Ida Snow James sang as a quartet. My sisters—Gertha, Peacie, and I—sang three-part harmony as a trio.

I wanted to learn to play the piano also. Since we had no piano at home, I drew a keyboard on poster board and practiced songs, reading the shaped notes, and then I would go to the church and play the songs on the piano to see if they sounded right. The first song I learned to play was "Jesus, Lover of My Soul." Later, when I lived in Wauchula, Florida, a family in the church offered to pay for me to take piano lessons. The teacher thought I knew more than I did. The song I played for the audition was "Lord, I'm Coming Home." I had practiced it well although ignorant, of course, of fingering, and technique. The music she assigned in my lessons was much too difficult for me to play. She thought that since I could read shaped notes, I could also read conventional music as well. Years later, I had voice lessons from a Mr. Jeffries, minister of music at Central Christian Church, in Indianapolis, Indiana, and with Susie Roerich in Tübingen, Germany.

In the spring of 1935, while we were living in Wauchula, Florida, Daddy's father, Pap, became ill and was not expected to live. Daddy took four-year-old Inell with him, leaving the other family members to work in the strawberry patches, and traveled to Lawley, Alabama, to be at his bedside. Inell remembers that Daddy gave her some crackers to eat on the train and told her not to let any crumbs get on the seat. If she did, he said, the conductor might take her home with him!

After about a week, Daddy became ill. (He had already been diagnosed with diabetes.). Inell recalls that irons were heated by the fireplace, wrapped in cloths, and placed in the bed to warm Daddy's feet. She was worried that they might start a fire and burn him. He died from colon blockage April 24, 1935.

We took the train back to Alabama for the funeral at Tabernacle Episcopal Church. He was buried in the cemetery there beside our mother. Pap, Daddy, and Inell had been staying with Uncle Coba's family (Uncle Coba was Daddy's brother, Pap's son.). Uncle Coba placed the following note of appreciation in the local newspaper for those who helped during that difficult time:

In Loving Memory of Orton Lawrence

Through the columns of The Press we wish to thank our many friends for the great kindness shown us during the illness and death of our brother, O.S. Lawrence, who was taken sick Saturday night, April 20, and the death angel visited him Wednesday morning at seven o'clock. The Lord needed another jewel in his kingdom and according to the testimony he left behind, he went to a place where there will be no sorrow, no pain, and no separating. His home was in Florida. Orton was visiting his father who has been sick for a month. He is survived by a wife and six children, two brothers, four sisters. Rev. W.M. Chadwick and H. W. Smith conducted the funeral service. I say again we wish to thank everyone that assisted in any way.

Now Mama was left a widow at age twenty-four, with six children to care for and no job. She applied for welfare and received $12 a month. It was raised to $18 and then $36. Even this was not sufficient to support a growing family and so, to earn some needed money, she sold Cloverene salve from her home and did sewing for people. She even made dresses for us out of flour sacks and sheets out of cow feed sacks. Back then, flour, cow feed, and chicken feed came in floral-designed cloth sacks. These were plentiful as we owned a cow and some chickens. Eventually, after I left home, Peacie and Gertha were able to get jobs in Selma. They gave Mama money so that J.B. and Inell could go to school.

Inell, mama & J.B.

In addition, when they came home weekends, they brought groceries to help with her budget.

Buddy lived with different families who tried to help him go to school and to do odd jobs so he could help pay for Daddy's funeral expenses. Finally, at about sixteen, he lied about his age and got a job in Tuscaloosa as an orderly in a hospital. He made good money and bought himself two or three suits. We all felt proud of him. He kept telling me that I could also do well "out in the world." Sometimes though, Peacie, Gertha, and I stayed with relatives. A couple of summers, we were invited to visit Aunt Vic (Victoria Gentry, Daddy's sister) in Tuscaloosa. Aunt Vic's two sons, Boyd and Fred, would taxi us around to their friends and have us sing for them. We sang three-part harmony and I guess, at our young ages, that was something unusual. Sometimes, too, our cousin Ruby who worked in a shoe store would buy shoes for us at a discount during our visit.

Years later, on June 7, 1989, another cousin of ours, Mary Ella Moore Henderson, wrote in the *Centreville Press*:

> I remember when I was growing up without a sister, one girl with three brothers…a cousin, Ottie Mearl Lawrence, came to live with us for a while….She became my sister I had wanted for so long. She had lost her mother when she was quite young and then she lost her dad. She had a great second mother but with brothers and sisters in the family to care for, she needed some help….Mearl became the one to share my thoughts with, one to whom I could be close, who was near my age. We shared a lot of love and good times for that short time and in the succeeding years….

Even though the area where we lived was somewhat isolated, sometimes gypsies would ride the freight trains, and while the trains were stopped in Randolph, they got off and wandered around in the community. Eventually, they would secretly get on another freight train and travel on.

On one occasion, a woman stopped at Mama's parents' home. She asked for food and inquired if she could spend the night. The word spread, and a number of us neighborhood children gathered to get a look at her. She was fascinating, for she carried a little guinea pig. She also showed us that she was wearing seven dresses! It was her desire to sleep on the floor, and so we slept on the floor around her. The next morning she slipped out and was gone. We never heard from her again.

4.
Ottie Mearl's Teenage and College Years

At age fourteen, my life changed dramatically. It so happened that a truckload of people were going to Wauchula, Florida, the place where our family had gone to pick strawberries in the winter time. Mama allowed me to go along. It was a sad day when I left my family. I wrote a note to Gertha and told her that if I never saw her on earth again, I would meet her in heaven. I had no idea with whom I would stay in Florida. Once there, however, Uncle Ben Rogers and Aunt Zettie, a distant cousin of my father, invited me to stay with them. They were middle-aged and had never had children.

Two things stand out in my memory during the time that I was with them: I was given a new Gene Autry guitar by Mr. Stephens, their friend. It was special to have my own musical instrument. Also, Aunt Zettie suggested on one occasion when we were having chicken for dinner that I wring its neck and pick the feathers. I tried twice to wring its neck and both times the chicken got up and ran off! By that time, I was in tears and Uncle Ben finished the job. I did scald the chicken and picked the feathers. It was not easy to eat it, knowing all that had happened to it before it was served on the table.

When school started for the year, I was placed in the eighth grade in the Wauchula school system. We had a wonderful principal. I heard her say to a student who had misbehaved and sent out into the hallway, "You can be whoever you want to be. There are no limits!" I decided then that I would set a goal for myself, confident that her statement must be true.

My brother, Elton, who was three years older than I, decided that if he were to quit his job in Tuscaloosa and move to Florida, he and I could live together in an apartment! He got a job in a local shoe store and we rented an apartment. In the meantime, the minister of the Christian Church in Wauchula where Aunt Zettie and Uncle Ben were members, Errett McCleary and his wife, Doris, began to show an interest in us. Doris came to the apartment and taught me how to cook, wash clothes and iron them. They actually became my legal guardians.

I began to settle into my new life which, of course, included finding a church in which to worship. Aunt Zettie had said that I should consider becoming a member of the Christian Church where they worshiped, but I had already, in my short life, belonged to two denominational churches; and I was not inclined to change again.

My first membership had been in the Methodist church. Shortly after my mother died, Buddy and I had attended a protracted meeting at the Cox Chapel Methodist Church in Lawley, Alabama. One evening, when the evangelist gave the invitation at the end of the sermon, Buddy went forward. He wanted me to go forward the next evening. He said he would let me know when the invitation was given and he would go with me. The time came. He nudged me and I knew it was time to go up front. The next Sunday we, together with several other children, were to be baptized (sprinkled) at Tabernacle Methodist Church where our relatives were members. When the time came, we formed a semicircle around the pulpit. The minister took a fruit jar full of water, and dipping his fingers in the water, he laid his hand on the head of each child, saying, "I baptize you in the name of the Father, the Son and the Holy Ghost." I watched him and, as he came to me, the last one, I ducked from under his hand and ran out of the church. Aunt Drudie had curled my hair and I was afraid the water would take the curls out! She eventually found me and led me back to finish the ceremony. Of course, I had no idea about the significance of what was happening.

After Daddy's second marriage, Mama, who was a Baptist, taught me that biblical baptism is by immersion. I inquired of the Methodist minister at Tabernacle if he would immerse me and he said he would, but he never got around to it. Then I asked the Baptist minister in Randolph if he would immerse me. He agreed, but told me I would have to become a member of the Baptist church. Hesitantly, I consented. A boy my age and I were baptized at the same time in what we called the old swimming hole in a creek between Lawley and Randolph. As I came up out of the water and ascended the bank, Mama was there to greet me with a hug and a bouquet of wild flowers—a precious moment.

Now, in Wauchula, I was being encouraged to become "a Christian only"—not a Methodist, not a Baptist, not a Presbyterian, not an Episcopalian, but "just a Christian." It was explained to me that the Christian Church emphasizes Christian unity on the basis of biblical teaching and living. Immersion is the biblical form of baptism, and each Sunday, members meet for Christian worship and teaching and to partake of the Lord's Supper. "As often as you do this," Jesus said, "you do it in remembrance of me." I was reminded that the first Christians met on the first day of the week for the breaking of bread and prayer. (See Matt. 26:26ff; I Cor. 12:23ff; Acts 20:7) I didn't understand everything, but I did understand enough to want to become a part of such a fellowship of believers.

When O.K. Cull, minister of Central Christian Church in Tampa, held a meeting at the Christian Church in Wauchula, I finally decided to become a member. I was at the point of really seeking the Lord for my way ahead and found secret niches in the church where I would slip in and pray. Not only did I want to become a member of that church, I wanted to give my life fully in service to the Lord. A young man in the church, Jake Thomas, also wanted to dedicate his life to Christian service, and in preparation, attend Kentucky Christian College. And so in a special service, the elders of the church laid their hands on our heads and prayed for our dedication to the work of the Lord.

When O.K. Cull returned home, he wrote me the following letter which I have kept among my prized possessions throughout succeeding years:

Rev. O.K. Cull

I am so glad I had the pleasure of meeting you and that you have come to be one of my best friends. There is nothing in this world like Christian friendship and fellowship. For years I have been giving my life to worthy boys and girls and doing all in my power to help them. If I had a million dollars I guess it would all go that way. But since I haven't the money I have to find other ways of helping them. Usually I am successful. You have a great spirit and a fine faith. Your ideals are high and there is not the least doubt in my mind but what you are going to make a great success in life.

The most successful life is not easy. It is always hard. A climb, a burden, a cross to bear and etc. No one ever climbed to the top without a struggle and by overcoming great handicaps. What others have done, you can do....You have many true friends who are anxious about your success and are praying for you and are willing to do anything in their power to help you. I want you to learn to TRUST GOD in everything and for everything. If He could answer the prayers of Christ He can answer your prayers. If you can grow a faith in Him that battles down all doubts in your heart and learn to trust Him in the darkest hours and most trying situations, you will have a peace that flows like a river through your mind and a joy that will not leave your heart. I am giving you some passages on PRAYER and FAITH. Mark them in your Bible. Memorize them until you have them at your fingertips and on the edge of your tongue: Mt. 21:22; John 16:24; Phil. 4:6; Phil. 4:19; Hebrews 4:16; Peter 5:7. These promises come from the Word of God. I know He is just as much concerned about you as He is anyone else on earth. If you find your faith failing you, then PRAY that you may be able to believe. PRAY for Him to increase your trust. Take everything to Him. Nothing is too small. I take every phase of life to him—everything I want and everything I must do and all I want others to do. He does not always answer my prayers like I ask Him. That would not be good for my soul. I ask for things I ought not to have and things that are not good for me. I ask Him to do things in ways that are not best for everyone. But He answers in the right way. Make your life a protest against doubt.... I pledge you my friendship and all the help I can be to you in any way. I am praying for you every day and I know you are going to find peace and joy and that your life is going to be a beautiful Christian life and Christ is going to use you in a great way....

Shortly after I received this letter, Elton lost his job at the shoe store, and we found ourselves homeless. Aunt Ruth Wallace, wife of deceased great-uncle Nathan Wallace, took us into her home. Then one morning she announced that she could not keep us any longer and we needed to find other living accommodations. And so we moved into an apartment. Buddy, in the meantime, had fallen in love with Tiny (Lillian) Ezell, a member of the Christian Church, and they were planning their wedding.

When Pastor O.K. Cull became aware of my situation, he invited me to go to Tampa and live with his family. Then, one day, Mallie, his wife, and their son, George, arrived and took me to their home in Tampa, saying, "We are family." This meant that I had two new brothers, George and his brother Allen, who were kind and inclusive. George, the younger one, was "Buzzie" and I was "Sistie," called after a couple of President and Mrs. Franklin Delano Roosevelt's five children. To this day, George's children call me "Aunt Sistie."

I am sure Mother Cull did not find it easy to take me into her home. She was already caring for her husband's mother who was bedfast. My bed was a couch in the family room. One night while I was praying, I had a vision: I saw Jesus walking toward me. Then He vanished. I took that to mean that He was with me and would be there for me on my life's journey. With this in mind, I was motivated to do whatever it took to receive an education and serve the Lord.

Rev. O.K. & Mallie Cull

I finished the ninth grade while living with the Cull family.

I recall that it was discovered that I liked to sing, and for a school skit I was assigned to sing a song with these words:

> Dear God, I need you awful bad.
> I don't know what to do.
> My mama's sick and Papa's cross.
> I don't have no friend but you.
>
> Them naughty angels went and brought
> 'Sted' of the boy I asked –
> A little tiny baby girl.
> I don't see how they 'darst.'
>
> And say, I wish you'd take her back.
> She's just as good as new.
> Won't nobody know she's second hand,
> 'Cepting' me and you.
>
> And pick a boy this time yourself,
> Nicest in your fold.
> And please don't choose him quite so young.
> I'd like him five years old!

Eventually, O.K. Cull (I came to call him "Dad Cull") arranged a scholarship for me to attend Kentucky Female Orphan School at Midway, near Lexington, Kentucky. He had, at one time, been minister of the Christian Church in Frankfurt, Kentucky, and so he was acquainted with the school. Jean A Boyd from Pittsburgh, PA, was my benefactor, and I corresponded with her during my years at Midway and beyond. She once wrote: "A tea room would be a fine place to do missionary work as so many people are lonesome and discouraged when they stop to eat and a pleasant smile helps as much as food."

Allen and a couple of others from Jacksonville, Florida, where I was living, were attending Lexington Theological Seminary and so I was able to ride with them when they returned to school in the fall of 1938 and to enroll at Midway.

I had been at school six or seven months when Mother Cull wrote: "Tomorrow, April 29, is your 17th birthday. I am mailing you a box of goodies. We hope you have many, many more birthdays; and as you grow in years, may you grow as your Savior did, 'In wisdom and in favor with God and man.' I know you will continue to grow in grace and with each year you will become a more useful woman and a more beautiful Christian character."

Almost every week I received a post card from Dad Cull. He wrote about simple things—their pet rabbits, the weather and youth work at the church. He could never have known how much these notes meant to me. Letters of encouragement were received from relatives and friends as well.

Mrs. Claudia Williams, my former teacher from West Blockton, Alabama, wrote:

> Hudson and I are really pleased that you have so much determination to succeed. We feel so glad to have you for a friend and put the utmost confidence in you. Your stepmother would probably feel hard toward me if she knew I said it, but I thank God that you left Randolph and also for your Uncle and Aunt [in Florida] who have removed one of our best friends, but we can't be so selfish as to wish to keep you in our midst when it is a disadvantage to you. Hudson just had to cry some when I read your last letter to him. He said, "I declare she sure does write a good letter. Everyone just gets better." Tell us all about your school, where you stay, etc. Don't be afraid to talk about yourself because we know you aren't an egotist.

Aunt Pansy Cox, Daddy's sister, wrote that she was glad my life was consecrated to God: "That is the only sensible thing to do. I am not a Methodist anymore. I am now in the Church of God, not the Pentecostal Holiness. We don't believe in 'tongues.' Headquarters are in Anderson, Indiana."

Ottie Mearl & Opal

Sometimes Mother Cull enclosed money in her letters. If there was nothing I especially needed, she suggested that I take some of my best friends to the drug store for a little ice cream party or any other treat and remember her while we were enjoying it.

I became friends with Opal McElfresh, and we started a Christian Endeavor group on campus at Midway. It was the custom for girls at the school to attend the local Christian Church. I was sometimes asked to pray at the service. In preparation, I used prayers from the Congressional Records as models. When I graduated and left for college, Ronald C. Morimer, the minister, wrote: "We are certainly sorry to lose you in the work of our church but glad that you do have the opportunity to go on to school at Butler. I nearly went there myself several years ago."

Since I was a member of the school quartet, Mr. Edgar Riley, the publicity director for the school, often took us with him to provide special music when he spoke in churches. It was embarrassing when he would introduce us as students from the Kentucky Female Orphan School, for we didn't feel like orphans. Actually, there were missionaries' children at the school whose parents were serving on foreign fields. I was pleased years later when the name of the school was changed to Pinkerton High School. Now it is known as Midway College.

Dad Cull always encouraged me to use my talents. He wrote: "Never neglect your music. God has given you that talent and you must dedicate it and consecrate it for Him." So I took violin lessons and played in the second violin section of the school orchestra. Knowing my love of music, faculty members would sometimes invite me to go with them when they attended orchestral concerts in Lexington.

I was so impressed with life at Midway that I wanted my sisters, Peacie and Gertha, to join me there. In addition to letters enticing them to come, a recruiter from Montgomery, Alabama, visited them and offered scholarships. Central Christian Church in Tampa, Florida, was ready to help them financially. In Jacksonville, Florida, the McClearys gave a shower for me. I wrote my sisters that I would share everything I had received in the shower with them before I left for school. However, Peacie and Gertha were content to remain in Randolph in their familiar surroundings, with relatives and friends with whom they were bonded.

Peacie wrote: "I will tell you about myself. I can't stay away from home folks that long." Mama wrote: "I will talk some more to the girls and see if I can make them know that it's for their good and not just to get them off from the place they have always loved. I am careful how I talk, for they may not take it like I mean it for them to." Another friend hoped they could have the opportunity of attending school with me. "God give them strength and courage," Mrs. Williams wrote, "to take advantage of all the good things that come their way." Our brother, Elton, wrote from Florida, sent bus tickets and some extra money and wired the school that Peacie and Gertha were on their way. After a week or so, they wrote him that they did not want to go. He asked them to return the tickets.

In their own way, they have achieved admirable goals. They have focused on living the good life which involved faithfulness to the Lord and hard work. Most of their children are college graduates. Although somewhat isolated geographically, their interest in and knowledge of world affairs is no different from people in other parts of the country.

August, 1939, Dad Cull wrote: "I am so glad you can visit your sisters. They will see a different Ottie Mearl than they saw last, not in character, but in culture and refinement and general demeanor. We pray for you every day. You are our little girl. We want you to definitely promise us that you will not let yourself get in need and want of anything needful without telling us about it. It would hurt us if we knew you were in need and would not let us know."

Dad Cull was adamant that I should attend the Florida Youth Conference in 1940. He wrote: "I will send you to the Florida Youth Conference as my daughter. I want you to know the Florida young people. I want them to know you. Aside from the school there, your home base and closest friends are in Florida. I hope that in the years to come you will contribute something spiritual to the Florida youth. Another reason is that I am an official and nothing would give me greater joy than for you to be one of the Florida conferees." George Cull, his younger son, managed a canteen at the conference and all the proceeds were designated to helping me at Midway.

Mother Cull wrote that she hoped that I could use my talent as a "hair dresser" to earn some money at Midway. One of the things I had learned to do was to "fix" hair. Each of the girls at school was assigned a duty. One of my jobs was to clean the room (mini apartment) of Miss Lucy Peterson, the principal. She not only paid me for cleaning her room, but also to wash and set her hair. Another girl did her manicures. Waves were the vogue then, and many of the girls preferred waves to just having their hair curled. Curlers were not used. Instead, I would screw up a bit of hair and hold it in place with a bobby pin. A head full of screwed up bits of hair, held in place with bobby pins, resulted in beautiful curls when dry and combed out. "Fixing hair" was something I had learned to do as a young girl in Alabama. Gertha reminded me that on one occasion, I had set Iris McGee's hair when it was especially cold weather, and her wet hair actually froze as she walked home! Fortunately, she did not become ill.

May Day was a big annual event at Midway. When I was a senior, I was chosen to play the part of Columbia, the main character in a play performed at the amphitheater on campus. Also, that year I played the part of Tillie in our senior play, "Tillie Listens In."

Meanwhile Opal and I were sending in applications to various colleges and were also seeking advice. Mrs. Riley, the secretary at Midway, felt that we were too young to attempt to work our way through college in competition with the world. Dad Cull wrote: "Unless you can see your way to go to Butler without having to go out to work, I think you had better take the two year post-graduate work at Midway. That is sure and safe. But your teachers are in the thick of things and know better than I could possibly know. Their advice is worth more than mine. I advise that you be guided by their interest and feeling for your welfare. Whatever you do, we will do the best we can for you. Don't make your decision too hastily. Take time and think it through. I will be glad to advise with you from time to time in helping you work out your problem."

Upon graduation from Midway, I received the following letter from a revered uncle who was active at Tabernacle Methodist Church and was the first Justice of Peace for Randolph and nearby communities:

> August 8, 1941
> Lawley, Alabama
> Dear Chile:
> I am trying to answer the most welcome letter I received a few days ago. I am nearly blind, so you will have to excuse bad writing. Dear girlie, if you could know how much your letter was appreciated by me, you wouldn't be so long about writing. I am so glad that we have a Heavenly Father who can put pictures in our minds, visions that call us on to greater things than this world can give with all its wealth. I trust your vision will not vanish but grow brighter every day until your soul shall be satisfied resting in the arms of Jesus in that Kingdom that shall conquer all other kingdoms.
>
> Ottie Mearl, I wish you could come back to Tabernacle and conduct services one week for us. I feel sure the sainted spirits of your father and mother would help you in the services and also Jesus. What a glorious time we would have if you could come down. If you can't come, send your prayers.
>
> Let me be one who wishes you comfort, joy and happiness. Will give a little advice. Learn all you can but don't trust in your book knowledge. Your success depends on what God reveals to you, not what He reveals to others.
>
> Finish work for God but remember it is not what God told others to do, but what He tells you.
>
> I hope these few lines from your uncle may be of some help.
> J.W. Edwards

Years later, in the early 1970s, after we had returned home from Germany, I was invited to be the featured speaker at a Midway reunion.

Chapter Three
Finding a Life Partner

1.
Ottie Mearl meets Earl

I graduated from Midway in the fall of 1941. As Opal McElfresh had graduated in the spring of the same year, we decided that we would like to go to college together. Neither of us knew how we could finance our ambitions. Fortunately, however, we received tuition scholarships at Butler University in Indianapolis. With one hurdle over, we applied for financial aid from the housing department at the university and learned that an insurance agent's family needed a student to help in the household for room and board. The family decided to take both of us. One of us slept in a room on the second floor of their home at 4466 Central Avenue and the other in a nice room in the attic. Responsibilities were divided and the arrangement was satisfactory for all. We babysat their three young daughters, cleaned house, and did the laundry and ironing. Sometimes we cooked and did sundry other things. We were treated like family, except, in our opinion, when the family entertained. Mrs. Craig had a button under the carpet at her end of the table. She would press the button with her foot and a bell rang in the kitchen where we were on the alert. It was a convenient way to let us know that it was time for the next course. However, this arrangement made us feel like "servants," but we were careful not to let her know that we were sensitive about it. Actually, looking back, I can understand now that it was a wonderful arrangement.

Miss Lucille Hanna, Dean at Midway, sent our transcripts to Butler and expressed her pleasure that Opal and I were able to stay together. "I am sure the Craigs must be very lovely people," she wrote, "but I feel sure also that you and Opal both will live up to their expectations and merit anything good that comes your way. You have always been such fine girls. We hated terribly to give you up. Butler is very fortunate to have both of you and I am sure you will soon be into your work there and loving it as much as you did at Midway."

It was obvious that we were above the Mason-Dixon Line, for there were black students in our classes. I wrote home about it. Mama responded: "I can't imagine how you feel with your mixed classes. I wouldn't like very much to have class with a Negro." Times have changed and I feel sure her opinion would be different now. Years later when our little deaf daughter, Jane, first encountered a black person, she let us know that she had seen a beautiful "chocolate" lady!

The McCleary and Cull families sent money to me occasionally which I shared with Opal who had no outside help at all. In addition, we were allowed to have jobs elsewhere. The first job I had while in college was working as a "car hop" for a restaurant. Although I was paid well in salary and tips, I had to give it up, for it was the hardest job I ever had. A young Butler University student I was dating would come to pick me up after work evenings and, exhausted, more often than not, I would have to ask him to take me straight home instead of joining him in some activity. Eventually, I was able to get a job at L.S. Ayers department store on the circle downtown and worked some evenings and weekends. Later I worked as a receptionist for a Paper Art Company.

Life was not easy, but we were determined to get our degrees and move on. Following our sophomore year, Opal became engaged to Ray Eiford, a Bible major, and they transferred to Cincinnati Bible College.

During our first year at Butler, Opal and I had become members of the Gospel Team under the leadership of Herbert

Wilson, placement secretary at the School of Religion at Butler University. It was made up mostly of undergraduate students. Sunday evenings we conducted services in area churches. I will never forget December 7, 1941. We were on our way to a church in Indianapolis. The car radio was on and we heard the announcement that Pearl Harbor had been bombed. Stunned and concerned about what that might mean for the future for all of us, we prayed as we drove along, inspired more than ever to present a challenging program that evening. The desire to win the world for Christ was uppermost in our minds. Avert Witt was one of the speakers that evening and he had never been more eloquent in his message that not only challenged but stirred our hearts to action. There was a rededication of our lives to do all we could to bring knowledge and acceptance of our living Savior to all people of the world.

One of the first things I did upon moving to Indianapolis was to find a church home for worship and service and I found it at Northwood Christian Church. Here, I formed a close friendship with Hylda Young Smith which has lasted throughout succeeding years. Her mother had charge of the children's department at church and invited me to work with her. It wasn't long, however, before another opportunity came for service.

E. L. Day, Marion county evangelist for the Christian Churches, who had started the North Tacoma Christian Church, inquired if I would like to help. He would come for me Sunday mornings and we would prepare for worship services in a house rented for the purpose. While Mr. Day did the preaching, I had charge of the worship services and taught a Sunday school class. Fortunately, we had a wonderful pianist and it was easy to work with her.

One Sunday afternoon, Mr. Day and I were invited to take part in a service with a black congregation in Indianapolis. As he was one of the speakers, Mr. Day joined the choir procession. I shall never forget how he tried but failed to keep in time with the rhythmical steps of their music, conscious that all eyes were upon him. Although I had worked some among the black community with Lois Fuller Rees, who later served as a missionary in Burma, together with her husband, David, that was the first time I had attended one of their services.

College had been in session only a short time when a program was planned for all Bible majors. It was then that I "noticed" Earl Stuckenbruck for the first time. He was a part of the entertainment, playing his musical saw. I never imagined, however, that he would become anything more than a casual acquaintance. After all, he was a second year Master of Divinity student in "classical honors" at Butler University School of Religion and I was a mere freshman at Butler University with a major in Bible. I was bold enough, however, to tell him that I enjoyed his part on the program.

At Christmas time, Earl was in charge of a program at the school and invited me to be a part of it. However, due to an obligation to baby-sit at the home of the Craig family, I sought him out with an apology that I was unavailable. I sensed his eyes following as I walked away.

In February, the School of Religion scheduled a valentine banquet, and I received a phone call from Earl. Would I like to attend the banquet and could he accompany me? We agreed on the date. He arrived in a taxi to pick me up with a corsage—my first. I was reluctant to see him again because I wanted to be a missionary and did not want to be dissuaded otherwise. Also, I did not want to be labeled "one of those girls" who was majoring in Bible just to marry a preacher! However, we agreed to spend time studying the Scripture together. He arrived for our first study session with a rose bowl containing a rose. Subsequently, at our regular weekly meetings, he would bring a fresh rose for the rose bowl! How could I reject this kind of attention? Still, I held out until he began showing an interest in missions by attending the Student Volunteer meetings.

Virginia Beven Hall, who later served as a missionary in India with her husband, Keith, and I started a Student Volunteer chapter on campus. Dr. and Mrs. Abram Cory, former missionaries to China, consented to be our faculty sponsors. For our programs we had book reviews about missionaries and their work, recent reports from missionaries on the fields, and sometimes we invited someone to present a challenging message about missions. When missionaries came through, we would invite them to speak to the group. It was on such an occasion that I met Isabel Maxey, missionary to Tibet, who was on furlough. I introduced her to Warren Dittemore, a student at the School of Religion, who planned to go out as a missionary. Several months later the doorbell rang in the night. It was Isabel. She and Warren had become engaged and she came to spend the rest of the night with me and to share her exciting news. After a number of months, they were married in Cincinnati, and both Earl and I participated in the ceremony. Sadly, they had been in Tibet only a short time when Warren became ill with typhoid fever and died. Isabel invited Earl and me to serve with her in Tibet, but Earl feared that he would not fit into that culture very well. Also my fear of heights would prove a challenge in that mountainous part of the world.

The Student Volunteer group generated a great deal of interest for foreign missionary service. In addition to Warren and Isabel who went to Tibet, Virginia and Keith Hall served in India with the United Christian Missionary Society (UCMS); Chester and Martha Kendall Parker also went to India with the Christian Missionary Fellowship. Martin and Evelyn Clark and George and Ethel Beckman went to Japan with Osaka Christian Mission. Grace Shoppe married Dean E. Rogers and they went to Argentina, South America, with the UCMS. Ralph Q. and Anna Mae Adams went to Paraguay, South America, with the UCMS. Dr. John and Mabel Ross went to Congo, Africa, with the UCMS. Also Dr. Harold Hanlin, a Greek professor on the faculty, and his wife, Alice, went to Truk island where he translated the Bible into the native language.

As for ourselves, Earl and I had read and reviewed a book about a Russian, Iwan S. Prochanow, who was born April 17, 1869, and died October 6, 1935, in Berlin. At first, we wanted to go to Russia, but realizing the restrictions on missionaries in that country after the "iron curtain" descended and cast its shadow over Eastern Europe, we opted to settle as close to Russia as possible, perhaps working with displaced Evangelical Christians, of whom Prochanow had been a leader.

Earl had a room near the campus. One day a young man came by looking for a place to rent. As he started to leave, Earl came down the steps from his upstairs room and the landlady introduced the young men to each other. To their surprise, they knew each other, at least by name. Warren Fredrick Mathis was a member of the Council Bluffs Christian Church, Iowa, where Earl's father had been the minister. He took the extra bedroom upstairs and the two became the closest of friends.

It wasn't long before Betty Jo Crowl, Warren's fiancée from Council Bluffs, enrolled at Butler University. They later asked Earl to marry them in their home church. After the wedding I received the following letter from Earl.

> Dear Ottie Mearl,
> The wedding was almost ideal. Only your presence could have brightened it. It was a happy occasion. Betty Jo was smiling as she came down the aisle. Warren and I could not conceal our delight. While the service was progressing the three of us were exchanging smiles. No florist helped with this wedding. The day before Betty and Warren had gone to a friend's home in the country and procured several dozen gladiolas. I don't think it was overdone; it was just natural. The church was packed and there were well over 450 people present....
> Throughout the ceremony a girlfriend of Betty's played the harp softly. That was a beautiful touch. Betty was taking everything in. Before I could finish the vow to her she had responded "I will." And Warren whispered to her, "Say it again." And Betty did, as soon as the right time came....The main thing about this wedding was the interest of the people, and the spontaneous love of Betty and Warren.

Summer came, and Earl went home to Topeka, Kansas, where his father was minister of First Christian Church. He let his parents know that he had a girlfriend who wanted to become a missionary. Although his mother had an interest in missions and missionaries and had corresponded with them and entertained them in their home while they were on furlough, she was not keen to have Earl go out as a missionary. Her dreams for her brilliant son were that he should become a great theologian who would influence the theological world with a campaign for Christian unity according to the Scriptures, and, she figured, he could do that best at some Ivy League seminary in the U.S. He took a course at a local college while he was home and we kept in touch by snail mail. He wrote to Warren Mathis nearly as regularly as he wrote to me, discussing his feelings concerning the missionary question.

Following their graduation from Kansas University, Earl and Harry were ordained for Christian ministry at First Christian Church in Topeka. Now, all four members of the Stuckenbruck family were ordained ministers although Earl had not yet decided in what capacity he would serve.

The time came when he felt that he needed to make a decision about a companion for life. He always shared big decisions with his parents. His mother wrote:

> Our thoughts and prayers will be with you this week as you are reaching such an important decision in your life. We know that Ottie Mearl must be a real jewel and we are so glad that you have found her. We have always felt that somewhere in all the world God would be preparing just the right girl who would be the companion you would need for the years ahead. When there are anxieties or worries as to whether or not the girl is the right one, you can always be sure that it is the wrong one. When it is the right one, there will be perfect peace and joy in your heart, such as you face, that your decision is a safe one. No doubt her admiration for you is as

great as yours for her. That is as it should be. We believe that together you can make great plans for your future home. May God bless you and be with you always is our prayer.

Earl sent pictures of himself and me to his parents. "We were so glad to receive the snapshot," his mother wrote. "Ottie Mearl is very good-looking. She is really pretty. She reminds me of Lucille. It isn't any wonder that you think so much of her. It seems to me that both of you are very fortunate. You need each other, and I know that you will both have a lot of joy working together in the years to come. We hope it works out that way."

For a short time, however, I responded to the attention of another young man who was majoring in religion at Butler. This became of great concern to Earl. In desperation he wrote his parents about it. His mother answered:

> You are constantly in our thoughts. We regret so much that you have had to face such a loss. Life is full of contrasts, of joy and anguish. It is often a very rough road. But as we rise above our trials and difficulties, we become stronger in character. We can better understand others, and we are more able to help them because of our own problems and heartaches. In doing things to make others happy and to brighten their lives, we can in part at least forget ourselves. We had been so happy for you in the thought that you had found just the right one. We were so sorry that the dream did not come true. It is such a shock to give up cherished hopes. But we know that you are big enough to take it as a Christian should. Through the miracle of time, the thought that she is gone will be easier for you to bear. It would not be right to continue to want one who belongs to another. Such thoughts must be crushed and conquered. We must not live in the past and wish for what might have been. We must set our faces toward the dawn of better days ahead. "Build a little fence of trust around today.

Fill the space with loving deeds, and therein stay. Look not through the sheltering bars upon tomorrow. God will help thee bear whatever comes of joy or sorrow."

It will no doubt take some time for Ottie Mearl to close up her going with the other person without hurting his feelings. She is very probably quite interested in you, even if she can't appear to be. Then there is the probability that there is quite a conflict in her mind regarding the thought of giving up her idea of being a missionary. All of that will take time to work out."

Fortunately, I was not distracted long and on September 4, 1942, Earl's mother wrote again:

We were so glad to have your Special Delivery letter with the good news. We had wondered if there might not eventually be some more light on the situation. We felt all along there was some possibility there might be some explanation which would show that the last chapter in the story had not been written. We just hope everything will work out for the best in every way. It will be nice for you to go and see her.

Of course, Earl shared the story of his love life with his friend, Warren Mathis. "How joyful I feel as I anticipate coming events," Warren responded.

Earl's parents, however, continued to feel that we should decide to serve the Lord in America. They became quite depressed about the prospect of our going abroad, citing health issues and anxiety for our safety. They even confessed that our decision to serve abroad affected their sleep and their work. His mother wrote:

We realize that you are faced with a very difficult problem. We do not want you to give Ottie Mearl up. If there could be a happy solution for all of us, it would be wonderful. If not, we would want you two to continue with your plans and let us make the sacrifice. We have confidence in you, and we believe that you will eventually work everything out in whatever way is right. Your life has meant so much to us through the years. It is our hope and prayer that the future years will bring you much joy and satisfaction as you continue in our Master's service.

I broke the news about my boyfriend to Dad and Mother Cull. She responded:

> I've been thinking so much about that special news you told us. To say it was a surprise is expressing it very mildly. In fact, it was quite a shock. Somehow I had not thought of you falling in love for a long time. In my mind that was something far in the future, and here it was happening right now. Well, my dear, I'm so happy for you. It's natural and right that you should love someone and I'm so glad your Earl is such a fine young man. I know he must be all you think him to be or you would not have been attracted to him. I know of no one in all the world who deserves real happiness more than you do. Have you met his parents or is his mother living? You mentioned his father. Has he told them about your plans? If his mother is living, I would like to write her and tell her what a wonderful person you are and how very lucky their son is, and how fortunate they are, or will be, to have you in their family. Would he mind? I know how mothers wonder about the girls their sons choose.
>
> I want to start a hope chest for you, and I hope you will not plan to get married before I can have something worthwhile in it. I'll try and hurry it up "just in case." I'm so glad you are planning to go on with your education for even if you never go on the mission field, you will need all you can get as a minister's wife. Don't be too disappointed if Earl should decide not to go, for you will have a wonderful field

in which to serve the Master if you are a pastor's wife (assistant). There are many opportunities you'd never dream of. Had I not been a pastor's wife, I wonder if I would have met you and had any share in your life, and that's one of the things I would not have wanted to miss.

My dear, there were so many things I had planned to say, but somehow I just can't put them on paper. Please read between the lines and know how glad I am for you and wishing God's richest blessings on you.

Their son, George, sent his opinion: "What's this I hear about my little sister having a boyfriend? Give? What goes on? Honestly though, I do hope that you have a boyfriend. It is only natural. Life isn't complete without love. It gives you something on earth to live, labor, and die for. He has to be a fine fellow for you to like him. If he is a friend of yours, he is also a friend of mine."

When Earl returned to Indianapolis for the school year, he was approached by Herbert Wilson, placement secretary for the School of Religion, who told him that Meridian Heights Presbyterian Church nearby was looking for an assistant. He wanted to recommend Earl for the job. Earl took the position and worked mostly with the young people. He was granted complete freedom with the exception of administering the Lord's Supper and conducting baptisms, the two doctrinal areas which differ from those of the Christian Church.

August 6, 1942, Dr. Arthur Holmes, professor at the Butler School of Religion, spoke at the Meridian Heights Presbyterian Church and afterwards sent the following note to Earl. "I heard such a general commendation of your good work there from half a dozen different people, that I thought your modesty would not suffer if you heard about it. Dr. Harry says you spoiled him with your readiness at every problem, saying: 'I think I know something that will meet that situation.' Next time you write your folks, along with my regards, transmit your thanks to them for a splendid inheritance and fine training."

Eventually T.K. Smith, minister of First Christian Church (Tabernacle Church of Christ) in Columbus, Indiana, and teacher of evangelism at the School of Religion, invited Earl to become his assistant minister. Earl traveled to Columbus after school on Fridays. During the weekends he "did calling," using his bike for transportation. Also, he planned activities with the youth. It was war time, and one of his sad duties was to accompany young men who were "called up" to the train station, have a farewell prayer with them, and present each one with a New Testament. This endeared him to the people in the congregation and they to him. When T.K. had to be away, Earl preached. The story is told that when the staff had difficulty locating Earl, they assumed that he was probably somewhere in the building praying.

Earl once wrote to a friend that there was a time in his life when he was not sure whether to continue his desire to be a minister of Jesus Christ. During that time of wavering, his life began to lose its meaning. He knew that something was wrong, but he could not right the matter by himself. When the moment of crisis came, it dawned on him that if God sent his only begotten Son into this world to die for our sins, then his life could not mean very much to God or to himself unless he participated in the purpose of God to reconcile all men unto himself through his Son. This revelation led to a time of yielding his life to the will of the Lord.

After this, opportunities of which he had never dreamed began to unfold. There were still times of trial and testing, but in so far as he pressed on, God strengthened and guided him. By the time he went to Columbus, he knew he wanted to serve the Lord completely, but he was not yet aware of the work the Lord had for him to do. As he continued in studies at the school, in Bible reading and prayer, in association with Christian people, ministers, and missionaries, he began to realize for himself how little of the world for which Jesus Christ gave his life had access to Him in accordance with his Word.

The missionary vision which now began to unfold in his life, turned its focus on the continent of Europe where, within a generation, two World Wars had erupted that were costing the lives of fine young men and dragging society down to the lowest levels of degradation and brutality. "It seemed to us," Earl wrote, "that the Kingdom of God could never come until the people on that continent are drawn together in faith and fellowship in Jesus Christ according to the simplicity and finality of the New Testament record. Together, then, we went on with our preparation and service until the time that our mission could be undertaken."(From Earl's diary)

Sunday evenings, Earl would take the train from Columbus back to Indianapolis. On his way home from the train station, he would stop by 4466 Central Ave, where I lived, and throw cinders at a window of my upstairs room. I would acknowledge his presence by opening the window. In hushed voices, we would exchange a few words, throw each other a kiss, and Earl would walk on to his room a couple of blocks away.

Christmas, 1942, in a simple little ceremony, Earl and I pledged our lives to each other. It took place in Earl's rented room. He read I Cor. 13, and each of us prayed for God's guidance in the years to come. Earl gave me a Gruen watch in memory of our decision. It wasn't until the next Christmas, 1943, that he gave me an engagement ring. Betty and Warren Mathis prepared a lovely dinner in their home to celebrate the occasion. In the meantime, Earl's parents had become reconciled to our missionary plans. His mother had even offered to purchase my ring on approval by Earl. However, while home during the summer, he had chosen the diamond at a jewelry store which belonged to friends of his parents.

Mid-way during the spring semester of 1944, Earl became ill. Both legs were swollen below the knees to the extent that he could not walk, and he spent time in a hospital. It was a strange illness, and it was never diagnosed. His mother flew in from Topeka. In sizing up the situation, she advised us to reconsider our plans for the mission field, and even our engagement. The doctors could not promise any definite good news for the future, but, somehow, we felt it was not the right moment to make hasty decisions. We were proven right, for the symptoms of Earl's illness disappeared as mysteriously as they had come.

When Earl was released from the hospital in April, he decided to drop his courses at the School of Religion, and return to seminary for the fall semester. Meanwhile, a friend, Frank Albert, needed help. He was desperately trying to finish his B.D. thesis so that he could enter Harvard in the fall and work toward a PhD degree, and so Earl helped him organize the material and even typed the final copy of Frank's thesis according to the Turabian Manual instructions. Their time was consumed with the project.

It was a stressful though happy time. Our wedding was coming up June 1, and there were many questions to consider. Earl was involved with Frank and pressed for time so I could not distract him. In succeeding years, I found that one of Earl's characteristics was that he persevered to finish any task he undertook, especially if it had to do with helping others. And I was also extremely busy preparing for semester finals.

After school had started in the fall and Frank Albert was at Harvard, he wrote to Earl:

> God pity us if we are going to depend upon scholars to save this world or do anything constructive for it. What shall we do? Well, again I say, Preach the Word! Build new schools! Send more missionaries! Recruit more young men! Publish a healthy and constructive brotherhood paper! . . . .
>
> I think we should never cease taking part in the Convention life, whether through attendance, contribution, or participation. We 'young ministers' will not be too young too long. The day will come when opportunities for responsible leadership will be open and if, as young men, we have been directed to affirm our faith in the Movement and

hope for its widespread into the world, then there will be no doubt in my mind that the future of the Convention as well as our people will be steered into the right direction.

2.
WEDDING BELLS

My wedding gown had been purchased months in advance of our wedding when I was able to take advantage of a sale at L.S. Ayers where I worked. Even so, the price had been more than I could afford. Remembering that one of the secretaries, Ruth Stone at the School of Religion, was planning her wedding at the same time, I inquired if she would like to pay half the cost of the gown and wear it for her wedding as it was to take place before mine. It was a happy solution for each of us. More than sixty years later, we reconnected. Her husband, Lester Piper, had passed away. Ruth was ninety-three and living in an assisted living facility near the campus of Kentucky Christian College where her husband had taught.

Since I was determined to pay for the flowers for our wedding myself, they had to be kept to the minimum. I was glad of this for when Earl's father wanted to know if I had run up a lot of bills which I expected him to pay, Earl assured him that I had no debts.

Finally, the wedding plans came together—just in the nick of time! Martha Kendall, the only girl among our student friends who had a car, drove me from my home to Sweeney chapel at Butler University School of Religion where the ceremony was to take place. A large number of students, faculty, and community friends were present. Virginia Wilson was organist. Since I had no one to "give me away," I started down the aisle alone, carrying a bride's Bible, topped with pink roses from which fell streamers of ribbons tied with sweetheart rosebuds. Earl met me half way and we walked to the altar together. Margo Ellerbrook was my matron of honor and Lucille Stuckenbruck, Betty Mathis, Marcella

Burton—School of Religion friends, and Mary Frances Morone, a Roman Catholic, who had to get permission from her priest to participate, were bridesmaids. They carried New Testaments, topped with roses with ribbon streamers. Earl's brother, Harry, was best man. James Ellerbrook, Warren Mathis, Avert Witt and Paul Burton were assistants. The ceremony was performed by Earl's father, Carroll Stuckenbruck, who was assisted by ministers, T.K. Smith, Errett McCleary, E.L. Day, and Herbert Wilson. Vocalists were Kenneth Stewart and Mrs. Harold (Alice) Hanlin. Three local newspapers carried the news.

Following a brief reception in the school's common room, we boarded a train for Chicago. On the train we met a mother and her young deaf daughter. Most of our time on the trip was taken up trying to communicate with the little girl who had given us a card with deaf language signs. We never dreamed then that we would be trying to communicate with our own little deaf daughter some day!

When we checked in at Stevens Hotel, Earl realized that he had forgotten the travelers checks he had intended to use for the trip. Fortunately, we were to meet his parents and Lucille Stuckenbruck the next morning at the train station when they changed trains on their way to Topeka. Earl was able to phone Herbert Wilson to give the checks to his parents who would deliver them to us!

Earl enjoyed putting his thoughts into poetry. He wrote the following poem about our honeymoon on June 2, 1944, while we were sitting by a lake in Chicago:

Honeymoon Memories

We went to big Chicago
For our honeymoon.
We thought no one suspected
Our love was then in bloom.

That night the Stevens bell-hop
Picked up our grips and said,
"Are you two folks just married?"
Our color turned to red.

Another shock awaited us
When we could not find
The Travelers Checks we counted on
To have a glorious time.

Next morning at the station
We looked for Mom and Dad
And brother Harry's wife, Lucille,
The only friends we had.

The crowd was thronged around them
At track-gate number seven.
They hoped to be among the ones
To board the Kansas Cityan.

In those crowded quarters
Her hand slipped into mine.
We never seemed to notice when
The gate-man said, "Train-time."

The crowd leaped into action.
A suitcase hit my side.
The gate-man yelled, "Quit shoving.
There's more room yet inside."

The seats were filled with soldiers
Who rushed in double file.
The last I saw of the folks,
They were standing in the aisle.

We strolled toward Grant-Park lake-front
Where all was calm and bright.
The gentle ripples sparkled
In the sun like stars of night

We were in no haste to move
From this delightful spot
Until a motor boat swept by
And splashed us on the dock.

This disregard of lovers' peace
Impressed us as unjust,
But we forgave the pilot when
He made a trip with us.

Around the Shedd Acquarium
We walked upon the rocks
Till others came and spotted us
As newly-wedded flock.

That noon we turned our footsteps
Toward an ice cream stand.
The fellow who received us
Believed not in God nor man.

This life was all he wanted –
Heaven a foolish myth.
Friends could not be trusted.
An enemy could be hit.

With all his doubts and failings
There was something good inside.
His parting word to me was
"Take care of your dear wife."

The Adler Planetarium
Was our last stop that day.
The dome displayed the heavens—
Sun, stars, and Milky Way.

As on the Arctic Circle,
We watched the midnight sun
Dispense its rays of daylight
'Round the horizon.

No light can be sufficient
For the day or soul,
Except it be high, lifted up
As Christ, who's in us all.

Chapter Four
Choosing a Mission

1.
The German Evangelical Association

Following our honeymoon, we returned to Indianapolis and our rented apartment at 118 E. 46th St. Knowing our intention of going out as missionaries, Burton Thurston, a fellow student at the School of Religion, had been in touch with faculty members and others who had either given or loaned enough furniture to provide for comfortable living, which included an ice box! What was more, everything had already been delivered to the apartment—a welcome surprise!

We both still needed to finish our degrees. Even though T.K. Smith encouraged Earl to remain as his assistant at Tabernacle Church of Christ in Columbus, we felt the need to have the experience of a preaching ministry. Earl accepted a call to First Christian Church in Montpelier, eighty miles north of Indianapolis. We would drive there Friday after school and return after church on Sunday evening.

The church provided housing and meals on weekends. Most of the members were farmers. The chairman of the board, Roy Spaulding, was a congenial man with a heart of gold, and he had a wonderful family. We were often guests in their home. He was adamantly against eating in the church building, but cooperated in every other way. The church grew and we grew. It was a valuable experience.

After preaching two sermons, teaching a Sunday school class, and calling in the afternoon, Earl was very weary on the journey home. And so he taught me to drive. One evening, however, he was at the wheel when we were driving home. There was a full moon. It was almost like daylight. We met a car coming over a hill that was being driven without lights, and we collided head-on. Fortunately, no one was seriously hurt. We were taken to a house by the side of the road. In shock and with bruises on one of my feet, our host suggested that I sip some of his whiskey. Not ever having had whiskey, and not knowing how I might react, I declined. Roy Spaulding, chairman of our church board, arranged for us to have another car.

While Earl was finishing up his degree, I taught Bible in the Indianapolis public schools. Teachers would accompany students, who had permission from their parents to participate in the program, to the nearest church for an hour of instruction. Dad Cull had written at the time I was hired, "The school officials of Indianapolis never did send me a questionnaire on you. You see, you were elected to teach Bible in the public schools on your own merit and reputation and not on my assistance." Evidently, I had given his name as a reference.

Years later, our youngest son, Loren, while a student at Butler University, was sitting by a gentleman, Rev. Florizel Pflediderer, at a symphony concert. They introduced themselves to each other. Recognizing the name "Stuckenbruck," the gentleman told Loren that he had once hired someone by that name to teach Bible in the public schools. And so Loren learned something new about his mother.

Earl, in addition to his school work and ministry at Montpelier, Indiana, was an assistant to Dr. Abram Cory in the Missions' Department at Butler School of Religion. It was of special interest to him, for his B.D. thesis was entitled: *A Summary and Evaluation of Cooperative Principles and Procedures of Disciples of Christ in the United States in Reference to Foreign Missions.* Several professors of missions in various colleges copied his thesis and used it in the classroom.

It now seemed the time to explore sponsorship for mission work in Europe. As a member of the Student Volunteer Movement, I had registered with the United Christian Missionary Society to go out as a foreign missionary. September 26, 1944, I wrote Mary Lediard Doan, vice president and candidate secretary of this society, and received the following message in return:

> Dear Friends:
> Thank you for your letter and accept my congratulations on your marriage. Since Russia is your chosen field and we have no work there, I fear we must lose you from our list. I know how great a field of opportunity Russia will present to you and our best wishes go with you as you work there. If there is any way in which we might serve you, we would be very glad to do so.
> With every good wish, I am,
> Cordially yours.

In consultation with Abe Cory, professor of Missions at Butler School of Religion, Dean E. Walker, professor of Church history at BSR, O.L. Shelton, Dean at BSR and others, it was decided to revive the German Evangelical Association through which we could serve in Europe. This association had been conceived at a meeting in the home of Dean E. Walker, Indianapolis, in 1930, following the World Convention in Washington, D.C. at which Jessie Bader, Secretary of the Convention, had invited Ludwig von Gerdtell from Germany to speak. The German Evangelical Association was incorporated under the laws of the State of Indiana, September, 1931. Among the incorporators were P.H. Welshimer, Charles M. Setzer, Hugh T.H. Miller, Homer Dale, O.A. Trinkle, Bruce L Kershner, W.R. Walker, Dean E. Walker and T.K. Smith (Year Book of Disciples of Christ, 1934, p. 89). Fred D. Kershner was the first president. The purpose of the German Evangelical

Association was to promote the cause of New Testament Christianity in Germany and on the rest of Continental Europe.

When it was discovered that Dr. Ludwig von Gerdtell had already caught this vision and had established an influential church in East Berlin, the German Evangelical Association was founded to endorse and support his work.

Frederick D. Kershner comments on his interview with von Gerdtell prior to the convention in his article, "As I Think on These Things" in the *Christian Standard* under the heading "Our Plea" in Germany: "We have just had the pleasure of a personal interview with Dr. Ludwig von Gerdtell from Berlin, representing what is known as the 'Missionary Movement among the Intellectuals in Germany.' We have been much impressed by the remarkable similarity of this program to the historic ideals of the Campbells."

As von Gerdtell played such an important role in establishing the mission in which Earl and I served, I have devoted the following pages to this remarkable man.

2.
Dr. Ludwig von Gerdtell

Ludwig von Gerdtell was born February 4, 1872, in Braunschweig, Germany, and died August, 1955, in Indianapolis, Indiana. His ashes are buried in Crown Hill Cemetery in the Mausoleum. The "von" before his surname indicates that he was of noble rank. He was, in fact, a Prussian nobleman and belonged to an elite corps of the German military responsible for the security of the Emperor's palace and grounds. Von Gerdtell's father and grandfather had each served as commander of the Potsdam Guard. He was slated to succeed his father as commander if he demonstrated capacity for the position.

Friedrich Loofs (1858–1928), professor of theology at Leipzig (1882–1887) and then called to Halle, was one of von Gerdtell's most respected professors. While Loofs was studying at Leipzig he had belonged to a group of students influenced by Adolf von Harnack, professor of theology there. After teaching some years at Giessen and Marburg, von Harnack was called to Berlin about the time that von Gerdtell would have been ready to enter university. It is supposed that von Gerdtell studied with both of these men, since German students have always prided themselves on being able to travel from one university to another to study with the "greats" in their chosen fields.

Relying on his own reading of Scripture and other primary source materials dealing with the early Church, von Gerdtell came to the conclusion that Church and state should be separate, that baptism presupposes a personal faith (thereby ruling out infant baptism), that baptism (i.e. immersion) is symbolic of Christ's death and resurrection, and that the Lord's Supper should be the central focus of each worship service. Such views were in conflict with some of the leading theologians in Germany, including Fredrick Loofs and Adolf von Harnack. When von Gerdtell told Loofs of his intention to be "re-baptized," the response was: "If you do that you may be right, but you're a fool." (Von Gerdtell told Earl this in a conversation.) Someone else (supposed by some to have been von Harnack) reminded him of the 17th century law forbidding adult baptism to nobility under penalty of banishment or death, to which von Gerdtell replied, "If that is the case, I will be the last of the Anabaptist martyrs."

Von Gerdtell's sincerity may be measured by the fact that he would be giving up most of his former associations and presumably fortuitous careers if he were baptized. His grandson, Dr. Michael Zoellner of Berlin, confirmed this. Meta, von Gerdtell's older sister, was married to Dr. Roedenbeck whose brother-in-law, Ernst von Dryander, was the main pastor of the Imperial Court church of Kaiser Wilhelm II, and President of the Evangelical Church Board (Lutheran) in Berlin. Because of these connections, Dr.

von Gerdtell could have had a very successful career, as seen by the world, if he had so desired, either in the military or in politics. Instead, he chose to become a theologian. This had its risks as few would understand why anyone would pass up such attractive career choices and might interpret such a decision as springing from ulterior motives. It could even place him under suspicion of aligning with the enemies of the state.

Ludwig von Gerdtell, "the renegade nobleman" as he was sometimes called, was baptized sometime after his marriage on January 31, 1902. He did not remain silent about his baptism but wrote pamphlets and even a book on the subject entitled *A History of Baptism*. This book, along with most of his other writings, is reputed to have been burned later by Hitler's forces.

In the beginning of his ministry, von Gerdtell went from campus to campus lecturing to small groups, but after several years he was attracting thousands. During the period 1901–1913 he lived off of the income of inherited property, money he received from lectures, and support that his friends and family provided secretly. During the 1920s, a business man in Australia, whose last name was Norman, regularly sent him financial help. Later in the 1920s, von Gerdtell identified himself with the Christadelphans because their views were close to his own convictions. They gave him support though he was never formally a member. For about five years he was a member of the Baptist church until they dismissed him because of differences of doctrinal views.

In the 1962 edition of the Encyclopedia Series, *Religion in Geschichte und Gegenwart,"* (Religion Past and Present—a concise dictionary of theology and religious studies), von Gerdtell is described as "a wandering speaker about baptism and also an author." Several of his books are listed—for instance, his dissertation on Rudolf Eucken's position on early Christianity, written in 1908–1909 in completion of his PhD at the University of Erlangen, and *Brennende Fragen der Weltanschauung für denkende moderne Menschen* (Burning questions for modern-minded people). This was a series of six titles published between 1905 and 1928 which examined dogmas and interpretations in a critical manner.

The work of von Gerdtell was interrupted by World War I. As a conscientious objector, he served as a medic from 1914–1917. After the war, increasing crowds came to hear him speak on university campuses. He was convinced that if reform was ever to come, it must be started among, and supported by, the intellectuals and students.

B. A. Abbot's *The Disciples, An interpretation* fell into the hands of von Gerdtell at some point along the way, and he decided to come to America in 1929 to investigate this movement with doctrinal views so similar to his own. Abbot introduced von Gerdtell to several leaders of the Restoration Movement: Peter Ainslee, S. S. Lappin, G. I. Hoover, C. G. Kindred, W. R. Walker, and others. B. A. Abbot got in touch with Jesse Bader, Secretary for the World Convention, who invited von Gerdtell to speak at the World Convention in Washington D. C. in 1930.

Upon von Gerdtell's return to Germany in 1932, it was obvious that Hitler was disposing of his enemies. Adamantly against the Nazis and publicly speaking out about the way things were going resulted in his lectures being interrupted many times by the SS during the l930s. Although the disturbances were often drastic, Michael Zoellner could not confirm that his grandfather had ever had an actual confrontation with Hitler, as some have believed.

In any case, von Gerdtell was now kept under surveillance. Realizing that his arrest was imminent, a friend working in the Post Office in Berlin kept careful watch over the Gestapo mail. At this time, all communications were directed through the Post Office; hence, all orders for arrests came through one place. The day came when his friend (possibly himself a member of the Gestapo) informed von Gerdtell that the letter ordering his arrest had arrived. Immediately, von Gerdtell left his family and home, riding on the train to Basel, Switzerland, third class, (nobility usually booked first class), and so escaping the Gestapo who searched first class carriages for him. He remained several months in Switzerland, corresponding with his family under the code name "Red Indian."

In 1934, on leave from his teaching position at Butler University School of Religion to study in Edinburgh, Scotland, Dr. Dean E. Walker and his family visited von Gerdtell's home in Berlin, but Ludwig had already escaped. Walker searched him out in Switzerland. He wired Fred D. Kershner, Dean at the Butler School of Religion, to ask if they could get von Gerdtell out of Switzerland, could he come to the School of Religion to teach. An affirmative answer came from Will Erwin, chairman of the board. Von Gerdtell accepted the position and remained on the faculty at Butler from 1935 to January 1, 1943, when his retirement pension became available.

Chapter Five
Preparation for Missionary Service in Europe

1.
Getting Started

World War II ended September 2, 1945, and we were eager to be on the field as soon as possible.

The German Evangelical Association was renamed "The European Evangelistic Society," so as not to limit our sphere of service, and incorporated under the laws of the state of Indiana. In 1946, Dean E. Walker was elected president, a position he held until 1974 when Dr. Robert Shaw, minister of Central Christian Church, Miami, Florida succeeded him. Warren Mathis was secretary and Herbert Wilson was treasurer.

Walker's association with William R. Robinson, principal of Overdale College in Birmingham, England, a college for training British ministers of the Churches of Christ, prompted him to inquire if Robinson would consider becoming a member of the board of the European Evangelistic Society (known eventually as EES). Dean Walker also inquired if Robinson thought that the Stuckenbrucks could enroll in the Selly Oak Colleges, a federation of educational facilities concerned with theology and social work and associated with Birmingham University. This federation included Overdale. Furthermore, Walker inquired what the possibility would be of Earl pursuing a doctorate at Birmingham University under Robinson's guidance. Since Robinson was an adjunct professor at the university, he suggested that church history professor, C.F.D. Sparks, could represent Earl at the university, and that he would accept the proposition to be Earl's "doctor father." Although neither Robinson nor Sparks had earned doctorates themselves, they were scholars in their own rights. In the meantime, we would be seeking a place on the continent in which to put down our roots.

Butler School of Religion faculty and students shared our excitement, but there were others who questioned whether we should include "evangelism" in our approach. We were convinced, however, that Mathew 28:19 and 20 are valid wherever we are in the world, whether it be America, Europe, or in the bush of Africa.

In order to obtain passports and visas, it was necessary that we be sponsored by an organization recognized by the World Council of Churches in Geneva. Without question, we could claim The Disciples of Christ as our sponsors. Earl's father ministered to a Disciples of Christ congregation. My background had been with Disciples of Christ congregations. However, in spite of the fact that the Disciples of Christ were our sponsors, some Disciples of Christ individuals thought it best not to include evangelism in our ministry. For instance, Earl's cousin, Jack Finnegan, well known for his book, *Light from the Ancient East*, had done his doctorate (Licentiate of Theology) in Berlin and reasoned that to include evangelism in our ministry on the continent might throw a bad light on our work as viewed by the World Council of Churches. But Jesus' commission to make disciples and his promise to be with us burned in our hearts as we focused on finding a location where we could work with freedom in evangelism and still have a relationship in conjunction with a university.

The first meeting of the board of the EES was held at the International Convention in Columbus, Ohio, in August 1946. Earl and I were appointed as its first representatives. The Church of Christ at Lock Haven, PA., pastored by William L. and Edythe Thompson, became my Living Link support and Englewood Christian Church in Chicago, Illinois, pastored by Burton and

Elaine Thurston, assumed the Living Link support for Earl. Additional support was raised by board members among other congregations.

At the close of a chapel service on Friday, September 20, 1946, Dean E. Walker, professor of Church history, A. E. Cory, professor of Missions, and O.L. Shelton, Dean of the Butler School of Religion, met with Earl and me at the front of the Butler School of Religion chapel for a private "commissioning" and to ask God's guidance and blessing in the pursuit of our Christian activities in Europe.

Dr. Frederick Kershner wrote in the *Christian Standard*, November 3, 1946, under the title, "Bread on the Waters," that about 30 A.D., "the Gospel was being taken by the Apostle Paul to Europe, whence it came to America. . . . Today missionaries are setting out to preach the Gospel in Europe." He named Guy and Thelma Mayfield as going to Italy and six others who were in training to go to Europe. Then he mentioned that "Mr. and Mrs. Earl Stuckenbruck, brilliant young graduates of Butler University, announced recently their intention to go to England for further schooling in preparation for missionary work in Europe. . . . Thus is America returning to Europe the blessing of Christianity which Paul first brought to Philippi, and thus to us. True is the saying, in Eccl. 11:1, 'Cast thy bread upon the waters: for thou shalt find it after many days.'"

2.
On the Way

In addition to our personal luggage, we packed other goods, including a chaplain's organ, in a large box and left it with Warren and Betty Mathis. It wasn't easy to find someone to pick it up for shipping. Finally, Florence Walker, wife of Dean E. Walker, charmed a local company in Indianapolis to get it to New York.

The *John Ericsson*, a renovated war ship on which we were to sail, was kept from sailing for six weeks due to a longshoreman's dock strike. Fortunately, we were able to stay with Earl's brother, Harry, and his wife, Lucille, in Springfield, MA, until the time of our departure.

At last the *John Ericsson* was scheduled to leave November 7, 1946. We still had to get the big box from the freight train station in New Jersey to the dock for shipping. Earl was able to rent a truck, but then there was the problem of getting it through the "strikers" and onto the dock so that it could be loaded onto the ship.

At 8 a.m., on the day before our departure, Earl left me with our car in a parking lot in N.J. After he had gone, I realized the gas tank was practically empty and I had a nickel in my purse! I remained in the car all day until he returned. Scary! But he was having his scary moments as well. Arriving with the big box and having no assurance that he would get through the picket lines to deliver it had its moments of anxiety. Luckily, he found someone to drive the truck to the dock and deliver the box. He paid the man $20 and returned to me about 5 p.m. We praised God for one more of many answered prayers!

At dockside the next morning to bid us "God-speed" were Harry and Lucille Stuckenbruck, William and Edythe Thompson II from Lock Haven, PA; M.S. Kitchen and Randall and Pearl Smith of New York. Messages in the purser's cabin included those from Earl's parents, the Butler School of Religion student body, Dr. and Mrs. Dean E. Walker, and Dr. and Mrs. Abram E. Cory.

Earl was assigned to the ship's hold with some twenty other men and I was in a room on an upper level with a dozen other women. Because of the swaying and pitching of the ship on the rough sea, we were ill most of the way and only met occasionally at the purser's desk. Feeling the need for washing my hair, I risked doing it in sea water, much to my misfortune! We would like to forget about that crossing, all, that is, except the joy of fellowship we shared with other Christians who were going to Europe for the purpose of distributing clothing and food to the people of war-torn Germany. Unfortunately, the *John Ericsson* burned while in New York harbor in March, 1947.

After nine days on the sea, we arrived at Southhampton. We watched a huge crane unload our big box. It roused the curiosity of everybody. Not only was it oversized, it was addressed to Earl (a title in England) Stuckenbruck. No wonder people seemed to be especially courteous as we joined the long queues to get through customs and other formalities. About a week after we arrived at Overdale College, where a room was reserved for us, our large box was delivered by men bowing and asking for "**The Earl of Stuckenbruck!**"

3.
England

For the next two years, Earl studied with Dr. William Robinson, professor of Church Doctrine at Overdale College and at Birmingham University. While Earl researched materials for his dissertation, "The Nature of the Church in the First Five Centuries," I took courses in the Selly Oak Colleges.

Occasionally, there were visitors from the States. Jessie M. Trout, executive secretary of the Department of Missionary Organizations of the United Christian Missionary Society, visited England in 1948. She and I spoke at a Women's Retreat for the ladies of Great Britain. She brought with her an electric blanket and transformer from Earl's parents which was appreciated as it was cold in the dorms. Actually, it was cold everywhere. Velva Dreese, a member of Earl's father's congregation in Topeka, Kansas, and a representative of the UCMS wrote: "We are so interested in your plans. Etta Proctor sorta opened our eyes. [Etta Proctor was a women's worker in Churches of Christ in Britain.] As we read 'Committed unto Us' and other accounts and heard speakers, we know a little of how desperately you are needed and pray for your wisdom and activities."

In lieu of Earl, since he was desperately trying to work on his dissertation, I was invited to speak in churches and to give one of the messages at the British Annual Conference held in Glasgow, Scotland, in 1948.

Dr. Robinson had been elected President for the Free Church Federal Council, 1948–49. The personal respect in which he was widely held plus his role as president facilitated for us personal contacts with foreign scholars and students in Selly Oak and with influential ecumenical leaders in London and elsewhere, as we sought direction in our eventual transfer to the Continent.

Needing access to a good library during the summer of 1947, Earl accepted the invitation of Eric White to minister to the Dalkeith Road Church of Christ in Edinburgh, Scotland, while Eric attended the World Convention in Buffalo, New York. This meant that Earl could do research at New College Library at Edinburgh University and we could, in addition to ministering to the church, enjoy some of the cultural events in "Auld Reekie," as Edinburgh is sometimes nicknamed. These events included a music festival, an Enterprise Exhibition, as well as a visit to the famous castle and national memorials of historic interest. We also climbed Arthur's Seat, a large mound at the edge of the city!

While in Edinburgh, we were invited by a Mr. Swanson, a member of the Dalkeith Road Church of Christ and vice president of the Edinburgh YMCA, to a Plenary Session of the YMCA.

At a reception for the delegates, where Dr. John R. Mott presided, we met Dr. Miloslav Kohak, president of the YMCA in Czechoslovakia, Dr. J.A. Pellar, a minister in the Church of the Czech Brethren and brother-in-law of Dr. Joseph L. Hromadka, Dean of the John Huss Theological Faculty in Prague who had connections with the university, and the secretary of the YMCA in Prague, Mr. Lawrence E.D. Aplin from the U.S. who was accompanied by his wife and daughter. In conversation with Mr. And Mrs. Aplin, Earl soon became aware of mutual friends in the States with whom he had been associated for many years in YMCA camps before going to Butler School of Religion. The delegates responded with engouragement, welcoming such a project in their country and courteously proffering their help.

Earl inquired concerning the degree of freedom allowed in Czechoslavakia to Christian workers, and they all assured us that freedom was neither restricted nor in jeopardy. Mr. Aplin said that the tension between East and West in Europe was not affecting Czechoslovakia as seriously as the newspapers in America and Great Britain would lead the people to believe.

Another delegate with whom we talked was Dr. D.F. McClelland, former missionary to India. He came to that meeting in Edinburgh from a tour through many countries of Europe, including Czechoslovakia. In Prague he had talked with Jan Masaryk, the Czech Foreign Minister. Masaryk had just come back from Moskow. In Moscow, Stalin showed Masaryk the headline, "Masaryk Breaks with Stalin," which had appeared in various newspapers in the States and asked Masaryk about it. Obviously, there was a question of trust in Stalin's mind. Was this tension indicative of what was to come? However, not considering the newspaper headline to indicate serious danger, we projected our thoughts toward settling in Prague.

In the fall of 1947, back in Birmingham, we began to study the Czech language with a Czech journalist who was married to an English woman. After some months he called to say, even before the news broke in the press, that Jan Masaryk had been thrown from a high up window to his death. It was likely the country would soon be building a "wall" to keep out non-communists. From information gleaned through channels only journalists had access to, he advised that it would no longer be wise to project our plans in that direction. The "cold war" was now on the horizon.

Meanwhile, Earl accepted an invitation to minister at Moseley Road Church of Christ in Birmingham, the largest of the Christian Churches in the city, for three months. Harry Johnson, a member of the church, asked if I would conduct a service for the promotion of Sunday school scholars on a Sunday afternoon. "We are passing through a somewhat critical period," he said, "and I am confident that you will be a source of real inspiration to us all." I solicited his help in selecting the tunes to be used with the chosen hymns because words to the hymns were in one book and the tunes, some of which were used for the words of more than one hymn, were printed in another book! And so we held the book with the words in one hand and the book with the tunes in the other!

We kept in touch with Dr. Abram Cory. In the fall of 1947, he wrote Earl: "What would be your judgment as to the Watters [Dr. Archibald Watters] taking my work here as professor of missions at Butler School of Religion? I would like to have a confidential word on it." Mrs. Cory had passed away August 2 and he was beginning to feel the wear of years. "She went just a few weeks before our 52nd wedding anniversary," he wrote. "She went in the same lovely spirit in which she lived and with words of faith on her lips. Among the last prayers she uttered she mentioned you both."

As the months progressed, Earl worked hard on his dissertation, especially since Birmingham University showed little signs of encouraging PhD students in theology. Two young men, who had arrived with their wives to study with Dr. Robinson—one with a B.D. from Brite Divinity School, and the other with his M.A. from the University of Toronto, were refused admission to the PhD program at the university. Prof. Sparks, head of the Department of Theology, had little interest in advanced theological degrees.

4.
Switzerland

Respect for Karl Barth, theologian of the Confessing Church in Germany, turned our thoughts toward Basel, Switzerland. Barth had transferred there in 1935, after his dismissal by Nazi officials from his position at the University of Bonn, in Germany. He was instrumental in drawing up the Barmen Declaration in 1934, which insisted that Jesus Christ is the one Lord of the Church and that the Church is obligated to obey Him only. Obviously, this was done in defiance of Adolf Hitler. In May, 1943, Barth delivered a lecture to pastors at Gwatt, Switzerland, at Thunersee on "Die kirchliche Lehre von der Taufe," (the Church's teaching on baptism) and insisted that baptism is properly an act of one's personal confession of the Lordship of Jesus.

Earl and Walter Fiscus, another American PhD candidate at Birmingham University and working with Dr. Robinson, visited Basel in the spring of 1948. They consulted with Professor Ernst Staehelin, Church history professor at Basel University, who encouraged Earl to plan to move to Basel.

In May, 1949, Earl turned in his dissertation and we moved into an apartment in Basel, Switzerland, at 48 Gellertstrasse, to explore further the possibility of settling there. Not long after we arrived, word came from Prof. H.F.D. Sparks at Birmingham University in England that Earl's dissertation had not been accepted. He, together with R. Newton Flew and W.L. Knox, were the examiners of the work. A doctoral dissertation in England is sent to top scholars in the candidate's area of research for examination. At that time, the M.A. degree was usually considered sufficient for a qualified scholar. As stated earlier, neither Sparks nor William Robinson, Earl's doctor father, had earned PhD degrees. One of the examiners was pleased with Earl's work, another was not, and a third was undecided. The PhD dissertation of Walter Fiscus, who was studying with Robinson and at the university at the same time as Earl, was also not accepted.

Jessie Bader, General Secretary of the World Convention of Churches of Christ wrote:

> I think, because four of our men failed to secure degrees from Birmingham University, including Walter Fiscus and Earl, in the future our preachers will go to Edinburgh. We will have four men there this next year. Edinburgh University is delighted to have Americans in New College, but it seems that Birmingham University doesn't care whether they come or not. In fact, I think they would rather not have them on the campus. I got this impression after talking to several outstanding leaders among the churches in Great Britain.

Dr. Robinson was a visiting professor at Butler School of Religion at that time and felt very badly about Earl's dissertation not being accepted. He stated that Earl had worked very hard and produced an excellent dissertation which should have been accepted by all of his examiners. He wondered if it could be submitted to a university on the continent. However, there was no time to consider the dissertation for reexamination. We felt we had to move on.

After a short time in Basel, we discovered that Staehelin, a church history professor on the Faculty at Basel University, was averse to an open discussion on the issue of baptism which Barth had raised in his lecture to the pastors. Sunday afternoons, we took long walks with the Staehelins and discussed a possible relationship with the university, Earl receiving students for work there under his direction. It wasn't until we presented the possibility of evangelism and establishing a fellowship for likeminded believers did discussions become cool concerning the idea of our working there.

At that time, James Crain, Disciples of Christ representative for Church World Service, came through Basel. From his experiences in handling humanitarian aid, he was aware that the existing unsettled conditions were prodding people as a whole to search for more certainty concerning their existence than previously. He suggested that we would do well to investigate access to some university center in Germany. Churches, universities, and society in general were still reeling from Hitler's dominance and were open to discussions about a genuine Christian basis for building the future.

Earl wrote letters to several Christian Church chaplains stationed with the U.S. armed forces in West Germany. Their replies were encouraging. July 10, 1949, Earl wrote to the Executive Committee of the EES stating that our efforts to make a way for a witness in Europe from Basel were uncertain and we would like to explore the possibility of evangelistic work and a relationship to some university in Germany. Since the war, some twelve million or more people poured into the western zone of Germany from the Russian zone and other countries to the east and north. Although we could not go into Eastern Europe, it seemed that Eastern Europe had come to Germany. With the approval of the Executive Committee and travel funds sent personally by President Walker, Earl undertook a three-week exploratory journey into Germany and visited several universities.

5.
Exploring Possibilities in Germany

Earl's journey in Germany included conversations with a number of Christian Church chaplains. Chaplain Albert (Rudy) Moss, in Karlsruhe, drove Earl to Heidelberg to consult with Richard Cheatham, chief chaplain, and then on to Marburg. There, Earl talked with Heinrich Frick, Professor of Theology, and recently Rector of the University. Frick remembered the stir which Ludwig von Gerdtell had created among students in Marburg after World

War 1. Earl could hardly visualize Marburg as a base for teaching with an evangelistic objective. He also considered it unfavorable because of its leaning toward existential theology.

Earl next visited Hamburg but could not consider it as a base because of a strong Baptist Seminary in operation there. Heidelberg was not chosen lest the Germans associate this effort with the USA military presence. Other sites which were investigated and rejected were Giessen, Goettingen, Erlangen, Freiburg, and Strasbourg.

Earl then visited the Director of the Church of Christ mission in Frankfurt, which was supported by non-instrumental churches in the States. Through relief work in Germany, they had begun an evangelistic program. About $10,000 had been used the year before in relief for university students, but few had taken an interest in the witness of the Church of Christ. However, as a result of their relief program in the community, a church had been started. They, however, would be unwilling to work with the EES for "they would be as distant from them as the Roman Catholics," the director said.

Several people at the universities Earl visited had recommended that he talk with Adolf Koeberle and Otto Michel on the Faculty of Theology in Tübingen. So Earl went to Tübingen and visited with Professor Koeberle who received him courteously. Earl was immediately impressed with the faculty's focus upon the Scriptures. He sensed a deep yearning among them to recover people for God through Jesus Christ. Koeberle firmly believed that this should be the Church's goal and that everything should be subservient to that end. "The task is bigger," he said, "than we can do by ourselves. If you can help with it, you are most welcome." In regard to the EES having a relationship with the university, he commented: "If you can make a contribution, you will be welcome." Understandably, however, Professor Koeberle wanted to consult with others about the proposed EES objective, namely that there be a partnership with the university in order that qualified students, studying with Earl, might be able to study at the university also.

In conclusion, we became persuaded that the work of the EES should be based in Tübingen because of its scholarly tradition, excellent library, and historic commitment to Phillip Melanchthon's peace-making recommendation to Duke Ulrich in 1537 that:

> "The Professor of New Testament is to lecture on the complete sum of Christian teachings and articles of faith." Although based on the Bible, this was the beginning of systematic theology. It is not surprising that such a recommendation should come from Melanchthon, since he was the first Protestant systematizer of theology. What was intended was systematic theology grounded in biblical theology, certainly not systematic theology using Scripture for proof-texting. (Harrison, 1985:12)

Upon hearing Professor Koeberle's response to his inquiries, Earl wrote the following to the Executive Committee on September 8, 1949: "Professor Koeberle is willing for us to come to Tübingen at the end of October...and to consider with us later the adjustment of an institute to the Faculty of Theology." A remarkable opportunity was opening before the EES in virtue of this professor's recognition of the value of mutual research, the result of which speaks to all concerned. In the Society's report to the International Convention of Disciples of Christ in 1952, President Walker explained:

> We are persuaded that an academic approach is the most strategic, one which provides access to the theologians with the facts and precepts of the New Testament which are of divine origin and universal validity, and one which invites

students of various churches and countries to investigate these matters for eventual evangelistic service. (Yearbook of Disciples of Christ, 1952:36–37)

Dr. Alfred T. DeGroot, who earned his PhD degree at the University of Chicago and taught in a number of Christian Church seminaries, was on sabbatical leave in England in 1948 for the purpose of doing additional historical research when we made his acquaintance. He became a life-long supporter of this primary method of Christian missions which was to be adopted by the EES. He wrote: "The purpose was to work with German scholars in applying the New Testament to present European culture at the university level. From this effort an indigenous ministry was anticipated." (Garrison and DeGroot, 1958:507)

Time has confirmed the rightness of the decision that the EES mission should be located in Tübingen. In the years which followed, the same courtesy, openness, and encouragement which we met with at the beginning has continued. All who entered the scene in Tübingen could not but appreciate being received with respect for any contribution which they were able to make as a result of research into the Gospel left by Jesus.

Chapter Six
Beginning of Our Ministry in Tübingen

1.
Our Introduction to Tübingen

It was far from easy to obtain the necessary temporary approval from both the French military and the German civil government. (Germany was divided into three zones: the French, the American, and the Russian.) In addition, finding housing in crowded West Germany and arranging for the transfer of funds from the USA to Tübingen were challenging processes indeed.

In the fall of 1949, we took a train from Basel to Tübingen via Stuttgart. In Pforzheim, a gentleman entered our compartment. Seeing that we had no provisions, he insisted that he share his sandwiches with us, even though food was rationed. Arriving in Stuttgart at 10:00 p.m., without hotel reservations, with a curfew in force, and with no street lights, could have presented a real problem. However, our new acquaintance and traveling companion, Rudolph Geyer, consulted briefly with his wife who had come to meet him. Then they invited us to spend the night in their home in Sillenbuch, a suburb of Stuttgart. They moved their two children, who were asleep, into bed with them and gave Earl and me separate rooms. We both slept on couches and above mine was a life size oil painting of Rudolph in Nazi uniform. Needless to say, I spent a sleepless night wondering about our hosts' intentions, but their gesture of friendship proved genuine.

When daylight broke, we could see the desolation of Stuttgart. Only a few bomb-damaged buildings were still standing. Temporary prefabs housed shops along the main street. How desperately love and compassion were needed—the kind that can only come from our Father in heaven at work through His Church!

The next day, we took a train to Tübingen and arrived after dark and a few minutes before the 9:00 o'clock curfew began. Eluding some drunken men at the train station who attempted "to help" us, we made our way to a nearby hotel of which Earl knew. While we were eating breakfast the next morning, a lady came in carrying some loaves of bread. The proprietor and his wife came out to meet her. Although we didn't understand the language, it was obvious that they were arguing. To our astonishment, the proprietor came around, grabbed the lady with the loaves of bread around the waist, and threw her onto the steps leading upstairs. It was difficult to keep Earl from going to her aid. Such was our introduction to Tübingen!

2.
The Proposal

Prof. Dr. Adolf Koeberle, our contact person on the Faculty of Theology at Tübingen University, requested that Earl write out a proposal that we establish a "center" connected with the University Community in Tübingen and submit it for the consideration of the Faculty of Theology. This proposal was submitted January 5, 1950, and read as follows:

> It is our object to teach in Europe unity of faith and fellowship in Jesus Christ according to the New Testament. We are convinced that unity of the Church is not to be attained without restoration of the Church upon the basis on which it once depended.
>
> The Church expanded from the beginning with faith in Jesus Christ upon the facts of his life, death, and resurrection, with obedience of believers in repentance, confession, and

baptism, with communion in the body and blood of his sacrifice for all men at the center of their fellowship each Lord's Day, with service of the saints to one another, and with ministry of the Gospel to others. One Lord, one faith, one baptism, one body, one spirit—in this oneness of faith and fellowship lay the unity of the Church however far it was scattered and in whatever places it assembled. No less for the Church of later times than for this early age does unity depend upon adherence to these facts and acts. Nothing can become universally necessary to the Church that was not originally distinctive of it.

Various tendencies have combined to disrupt the unity of the Church. One has been to intrude theological opinions upon acceptance of these facts and observance of these acts; a second to discard or displace practices which were instituted with Apostolic authority; a third to make omission or commission of other practices essential to fellowship in Christ; a fourth to reduce the New Testament Church to a cohesive system of government or cooperation; and a fifth to claim access to true doctrine and practice alone through a particular tradition of the Church or succession within it.

These tendencies can be overcome if the Church is referred continually to the source of its unity. Those who thus consent to these facts of faith and acts of fellowship in Jesus Christ should then proclaim them for obedience of others to Christ, and for fellowship which retains the original unity of the Church in Him.

Both of these tasks are envisioned in the mission of teaching for which we have come to Europe. To this end we should like to receive students in Tübingen who would be assisted also, according to qualification, to study in the Faculty of Theology. It is our intention also to give help to other students than those with us.

We are undertaking this work on behalf of churches in the United States known as Christian Churches or Churches of Christ, whose members number around 1,800,000. On account of one convention of their members, the International Convention of Disciples of Christ, they are often called Disciples of Christ, but as members of the Church, the Body of Christ, they adopt no official name, and consent alone to scriptural names as Christians, brethren, saints, or disciples. As in name, so also in practice, these churches desire to be distinguished by that alone which is relevant to the Church universal. It is regarded that nothing more or less than what was necessary for obedience to Christ and fellowship in Him in the Apostolic Church according to the New Testament should be obligatory today. It is regarded that as a Christian anyone is entitled to preach, teach, preside at the Lord's Table, and baptize. Members of each church have freedom to participate in various committees, societies, institutions, and conventions among themselves and with other churches.

Though by far the largest number of Christian Churches and Churches of Christ is in the United States, churches of this type are not peculiar to this country alone. Arising for the most part independently of the United States, there are similar churches in Great Britain, in countries of Eastern Europe, and even spreading to all continents so that there is now a world-wide fellowship of over six million people. No system of government, either ministerial or representative, exists over the churches which are, in many respects, diverse. However, they are singularly united in their devotion to the essential nature of the Gospel and of the Church of Christ according to the New Testament. They are also united in their goal to recover unity in Christendom and to evangelize the world.

3.
Our First Home and the Birth of Earl Lee

It wasn't long until we found a room (twenty-five square meters) and shared bathroom and kitchen with the Herman Lang family. In the days which followed, we began to make daily adjustments to life in a city that we would call home for the next eighteen years. Although I had begun to study German in Basel, my domestic vocabulary improved considerably as I met Frau Lang and other family members in the kitchen throughout each day. They seemed to enjoy being my teachers and I was comfortable to learn from them. Although the family spoke Schwaebisch, the local dialect, they made a special effort to speak Hoch Deutsch (correct German) with us. To improve his German, Earl met in the evenings with the Lang family for conversation, and at other times with a professional teacher.

There were restrictions to be observed. Lights were supposed to be turned off at 10:00 o'clock p.m. We were allowed to take baths only once a week. In order to have hot water for baths, we had to build a fire under a tank of water in the bathroom. One evening, we were in the process of bathing when the water tank became too hot and burst! Not knowing how to contain the flood, we quickly grabbed our clothes and called for help. By that time, the water had run out of the bathroom and down the hallway. The whole family became involved in mopping up the spill. Not on good terms with the landlord who lived upstairs, Herr Lang had to slip the tank out by night to have it repaired and then returned it the same way. We paid for the damage.

Tübingen had a chaotic population of displaced persons in addition to the "Einwohner" (local inhabitants) and despair was rampant everywhere. This, however, provided ample opportunity for the work of the EES which, in the beginning, included a variety of services. One such service was the distribution of food and clothing sent by churches in the United States. This gesture of goodwill not only helped to meet the needs of people but also opened many doors. This ministry acted as a supplement to the Hoover soup lines and was another means of serving God.

Frau Lang tells a story about Earl and some gift parcels. The customs' office sent notice one day that three or four large parcels had arrived and needed to be picked up. The weather was cold. There had been an ice storm and it was dangerous to go outside at all. How could we get the parcels? Frau Lang looked out her window about midday and saw a strange sight. Earl had gone for the parcels, had tied them together with ropes, and was dragging (sliding) them home along the ice covered street! He had found a solution!

We talked with people wherever we went: in lines at the post office, in grocery stores, waiting for buses, and at the customs office. As we talked, we discovered that some of the people were displaced persons, some were refugees, and still others were natives of the city or area. It was not unusual to see a family sitting by the Neckar River with one of them dividing a loaf of bread or to see lines of people in Hoover soup queues. Our hearts were heavy. There were only limited supplies to donate to the many who were trying to keep body and soul together. Some people approached us out of need for food and clothing, others because of our nationality, and still others because of our Christian concerns. As Americans and Christians, more was expected of us.

Soon a few adults wanted to know if they could meet regularly with us for Bible study, prayer, and praise. It was as though they expected us to disseminate the hope for which they longed, and it was a great joy to share our love for Jesus, the HOPE of the world. It was not that they were hearing the Gospel of Jesus Christ for the first time. In theory, they knew about it, but its application to life was often missing. By this time, we had realized, too, that we longed for Christian fellowship and that we could not work in a vacuum. It was important to help others who were struggling to find their way in a disrupted, family-scattered, and disoriented society. Our spiritual health, however, also depended upon fellowship around the Lord's Table with other believers.

One of the Lang children—second-grader Gudrun—had a birthday. It occurred to us that it would be fun and a way of contacting families if we planned a party for her and held it in a room adjoining ours, from which a "buro" (office) had just moved out. Gudrun was encouraged to invite her school friends to the party and so some twenty children came dressed in their Sunday best on a Saturday afternoon.

How to entertain them was a real question! I remembered that we had brought a flannel-graph board and figures for Bible stories. Using visual aids would enable me to communicate through my limited German and perhaps the children would enjoy helping tell the stories since they were taught Bible in the public schools. It was a huge success. They loved the stories. After eating birthday cake, I asked if they would like to have some more Bible stories in the future. "Ja, Ja," they said. And so it was arranged to meet on Saturday afternoons in a room at the Hotel Krone for more story-telling. A number of children came and a couple of adults. We learned German songs and, unknown to them and us at the time, the Christliche Gemeinde (Christian Church) in Tübingen was in its embryonic stage.

At the same time that we were adding to our circle of friends and to our Christian family, a son, Earl Lee, was born January 23, 1950. As far as anyone knew, he was the first American to be born in the Tübingen Frauen Klinik (Women's Clinic). It was necessary to present a marriage certificate to the authorities at the Klinik to confirm our marriage! Since we had been in the country only a short time and my German was limited, Magdalene Ketting was assigned as my special nurse because she could speak some English. I was given strong coffee and Broetchen (bread) for more than twenty hours so that I would have strength for the birth. Up and down the stairs and through the Klinik corridors, with intermittent periods of rest, Magdalene escorted me.

At 9 a.m., January 23rd, father Earl was walking to the Klinik in brilliant sunshine. Surely this is going to be a wonderful day, he mused. At that very hour the miracle of birth took place. All the nurses wanted to see the little American baby and Earl was in on the act, for he and baby were allowed in my room at all times. For ten days, baby Earl Lee was held, loved, and cared for in the Klinik. On the day of our departure for home, several nurses gathered round to have their picture taken with him.

Waiting at "home" in our one room divided into two by a curtain, were American missionaries to the Congo, Dr. John and Mabel Ross and their eighteen-month-old son, Ernie. They had been studying French in Belgium and would be going soon to Zaire under the auspices of the United Christian Missionary Society (hereafter designated UCMS). As a physician, John, and Mable also, were able to help us know better how to care for our baby, Earl Lee, in a foreign country. Our two families were together in the one room for several days. It was a time of sharing dreams for building a better world through Christian teaching and medical help—a time of seeking guidance, praising the Lord for the privilege of serving Him, and for contemplating and anticipating what lay ahead.

"Schwester" (the German title for a nurse) Magdalene, was a frequent visitor in "our home" to check on baby Earl Lee. Eventually, she went to India as a missionary nurse. We heard no more from her until our youngest son, Loren, was studying in Tübingen on a Fullbright Scholarship in the 1980s. Returning from lectures at the University by bus one day, Loren found himself sitting beside her. Upon introduction, she recognized the name and learned that he was a son of the family she had earlier known. In the meantime, she had returned to Tübingen and at sixty-seven years of age was a theological student at the University, learning Hebrew, Greek, and etc. with the younger generation. Because she was a student alongside young Loren, she invited him to be a "Du" (close) friend!

In time, it became clear that we could not confine ourselves to an academic work alone. The scars of war were evident on the faces of people we met. They could not be ignored. Ordinarily, people in Baden-Wurtemberg are known to be quite conservative, but foreigners, especially, seemed to appreciate contact with others. We spoke to them about hope for the future in the Lord and about our plans for living in Germany. We wanted to share the good news of God's presence which gives hope—something to live for and assurance that Christ is alive and is the same yesterday, today and forever—the one stable factor in life.

One day, a letter came from Paul Bajko. James Gray, warden of Overdale College in Birmingham, England, had suggested he get in touch with us. He came to Tübingen and told us his story. He was the son of Grzegorz, presbyter of the Church of Christ congregation in Targoszyce, in the Polkesie region of Poland. The Church was a part of the great Evangelical Movement for New Testament Christianity which had spread rapidly in Russia and Poland. At sixteen, while in high school, Paul accepted Christ as Lord of his life. When he was twenty-two, he was sent to forced labor in Germany where he worked in a factory and preached the Gospel to his fellow countrymen. A graduate of the Slavic Evangelical-Baptist Seminary in Germany, he became president of all the Slavic Evangelical Young People's Societies. These organizations held prayer-meetings and evangelistic campaigns in more than one hundred Displaced Persons Camps.

Neither Paul nor we knew each other's language. We knew a little German and Paul knew a little English, but not enough to really communicate adequately. Dictionaries helped. I passed by the door where Earl and Paul were visiting. Both were on their knees by the couch, each praying in his own language—their hearts united. Through the third person, Jesus Christ, there were no communication problems! Paul had become a minister and wanted to immigrate to the States. In 1950, Earl arranged for him to enroll at Eastern Christian Institute in New England where M.S. Kitchen was president.

Even without adequate facilities, Earl was eager to begin receiving students. In March, 1950, Ehrfried Frank, who had been led to Jesus Christ by Chaplain James Miller of the Armed Forces, and Christa Birkholz, Ehrfried's fiancée, a trained Kindergarten teacher, arrived in Tübingen to study with Earl and for Ehrfried to study also in the Faculty of Theology. He had had one semester already at Erlangen University. It was the desire of Ehrfried and Christa to enter into fulltime Christian service. Classes with Earl were held in our one room; and since students were not allowed to cook in their rooms and food was scarce and expensive, most of their meals were taken with us as well. It was not easy. Not only was there a new baby to care for, but there was no way to keep perishable food, and so it took a couple of hours each day to shop for fresh supplies.

Our plan, meanwhile, was to assist needy students in the Faculty of Theology at Tübingen University financially and with food and clothing sent from the States. If we were to have a partnership with the University, it was only natural that we try to be of help in any way that we could during those difficult times. But, in order for more students to be able to come to crowded Tübingen to study with Earl, it would be necessary to have a residential building with adequate academic facilities. We began to search for land on which to build. Funds for this were not available, but we kept talking with our *Father* about it. Back in the States, EES board members were aware of the need and were also talking with our *Father* about it.

On the political side, we were being watched by people who were reporting our activities to Communist headquarters in Berlin weekly, and so it was critical that we not become involved in politics. It didn't take long, however, for suspicion to lessen, but we were still looked upon with caution.

During the First World War, the Disciples of Christ had sponsored the "Men and Million Movement," led by Dr. Abram Cory, for their various agencies and projects. $50,000 of the money was raised to help Evangelical Christians in Eastern Europe—

particularly the group connected with the Prokanow Movement in Russia. Due to political changes in that country, the money was never used for that purpose. Instead, much of it was used by the UCMS (United Christian Missionary Society) to prepare missionary recruits for service on foreign fields.

When the European Evangelistic Society was formed, Dr. Abram Cory, a member of the EES Board who helped to raise the funds for the UCMS, felt that the money designated for the Prokanow Movement should now be used for the work of the EES. In the meantime, the Disciples had launched a "Crusade for a Christian World" campaign. It is not certain whether the sum of $13,071.42, paid in installments to the EES, came from funds that were never used from the Men and Million Movement or whether it was money from the Crusade for a Christian World. The amount donated was a disappointment for Dr. Cory who had wanted the entire $50,000 appropriated for the use of the EES. $6,500 of the amount given was used to purchase, in two transactions, a piece of land totaling 100 x 35 square meters on the southeast side of town with the option to buy more when money became available. Lois Lorack completed the purchase in 1951 while we were on furlough.

We had become acquainted with Lois, a graduate of Phillips University, when she came through Basel with a tour group in 1949 while we were still living in the city. She wrote that she would like to do mission work in Germany. We responded that we would be pleased to have her work with us in Tübingen if she could find churches that would provide financial support. She was able to join us September 4, 1950. Her sunny disposition lifted the spirits of all, and soon she was handling the German language well enough to look after Earl Lee, who was just recovering from chickenpox, while we accepted an invitation to tour places of interest in a number of German and French cities.

The invitation came from Wolfgang Nauck and his wife. Wolfgang was an assistant professor of theology (Repetent—tutor) in the Stift, a reformed college in Tübingen. Dr. Nauck's father, a policeman, was still a prisoner of the Russians in East Berlin and had kept himself alert by teaching Greek to fellow prisoners. In the mid 1950s, all the bells in the churches rang out about two o'clock one morning. Wolfgang Nauck's father had been freed and had arrived in Tübingen. There was great rejoicing among all the people.

After visiting several cities with the Naucks, from Colmar in France we drove through Freiburg, Germany. The trip was bittersweet in many ways. We experienced pangs of remorse and even guilt as we viewed the devastation caused by Americans during the war. This was especially the case in Freiburg where people were still living in rooms with a wall missing! We were relieved, however, when we read in a Tübingen newspaper a few weeks later that Freiburg had actually been bombed by the Germans themselves who thought they were bombing Colmar across the river in France!

4.
Changes

Things were generally going well with the work in Tübingen, but we were totally exhausted. Living in one room and having insufficient funds, either to help needy people around us or to erect a college building, left us wondering what to do. There were no funds to even pay the architect, Artur Achstetter, who had drawn up plans for the college. In addition, another child was on the way. Earl expressed our frustrations in a letter to Dr. Walker.

We hoped the EES Board and church friends and supporters would understand that we could not continue the work in one room; yet, it was questionable, even if we could gather the funds at this time, as to whether we should build a college because of the Korean War and anxiety that the Russians might invade Germany. However, unless we built, Earl wrote, there was practically no possibility of enlarging our accommodations. The housing authority let us know that there were 800 people ahead of us on the waiting list. A building would need to be approved on all sides, including approval from the Roman Catholic church across the street from our land. Without a building, we were at a loss as to how to proceed. We wanted to remain as long as possible in this work which we knew could gradually expand through good will and communication with interested people.

Earl had talked with three students who were interested in joining our efforts. He had baptized a Lutheran pastor from Latvia, who finished his medical studies in the University of Tübingen, and also his wife. Foreigners in Germany were more inclined to evaluate their lives in view of the future than "Einwohner." In spite of the fact that we had a dedicated EES Board working with us in the U.S., we often felt quite alone as we wrestled with questions about the future.

At this point, we remembered a letter from Harold G. Barr, director and Dean of Kansas School of Religion at the University of Kansas written in January 1950:

> If you do find that the handicaps to carry on such a program are more than can be overcome, I am sure there are still great opportunities elsewhere. Having worked now at the University of Kansas for thirteen years, this type of situation appears to me as one of the greatest opportunities of Christian service. You remember that I wrote you a good while ago about the possibility of your coming here. In a quite different manner, that situation may be open again this coming fall. Our work here is increasing and I have the feeling that we should plan to put on another full-time teacher. In the cooperative arrangement by which any religious body may teach courses here, there are six of us now teaching, but I am the only one giving his full time. I do not see any immediate prospects that the other religious bodies are going to contribute more than part time service. Eventually it seems to me that we should employ someone to direct the student work of the

Christian Church here at the university and also teach courses in our regular curriculum. Both because of your fine training and your knowledge of this type of situation, I know you would be particularly qualified.

As tempting as Mr. Barr's proposal might seem, we had made a commitment to carry out the pioneer vision of the EES in Europe. We believed that we were where God wanted us to be, doing the work He wanted us to do. It was a particular characteristic of Earl to complete any task assigned to him and, of course, I complied.

Earl suggested that we transfer Erfried, Christa, and three Latvian students to some college in the States for a couple of years while the political situation in Europe stabilized and the EES raised funds for a college. But, alas, there were no funds to even do that; in addition, the State Department was denying student visas.

It was very evident that we had reached a crisis. Important decisions had to be made. In September, 1950, Dr. Walker wrote:

> My two dear people:
> Perhaps I should say three for I suppose the baby ought now be included in all our thinking. Mrs. Walker and I are profoundly happy in the increase in your family, as I think you already know, and I want to take this opportunity to express my hope that you are finding great joy in parenthood.
>
> I think I ought to assure you that the living quarters in which you have been confined for these many months have given all of us much concern. We are profoundly regretful that there seems to be no way of alleviating this condition. Therefore, I want to urge upon you the very deepest consideration whether it might not be advantageous for you to return to this country for a year of recuperation and rest before trying to carry on in the face of such adversity. Probably you would find it possible to present the matter to a number of churches while here, and thereby be able to get hold of some funds with which to construct a suitable cottage for

yourselves in Tübingen. Or an alternative would be to buy a portable house here and ship it there. I do not know what this would cost but it is one possible way out of the difficulty. You will know better than I whether this is feasible and upon your return we could talk it through from every standpoint and thus come to some decision.

I am very deeply concerned, however, about the probability of an armed invasion of Germany by other powers. Now to this end I have written to the State Department and have received a reply from them, a copy of which I enclose with this letter. I give it to you though I am sure there is nothing particularly new to you in it. . . . It is not a question of vacating in the face of a threat; it is a question of whether remaining there in the face of such an event would constitute a wise and profitable course. In my own judgment, it would not. But we do not want to take action as a committee until we hear definitely what your decision would be in respect to the problem of continuing, as you look upon it from this single aspect.

Before we assemble in Oklahoma City it would seem to me most highly desirable that we have your judgment in respect to three points. In the first place, you have already expressed your opinion that you will not be able to continue in the present quarters and I am in entire sympathy with that position. In the second place, we do not know what your thought is in respect to the threatened disturbance to the world's peace. We would like to be informed on that question. And thirdly, we are unable to determine exactly what the status of the building, itself, is. We understand that you have possession of the property but we do not clearly discern the status of the building program.

I believe the fourth problem is that which will relate to the students which you have gathered, and the others with whom you have made friendly contacts. You have stated very clearly that if we could find a place for these people in some educational institutions, that it might solve the problem. This we will endeavor to do. It will take a little time, however, in order to see just how far we can go in this regard. . . . I appreciate very much your analysis of the possibilities. . . .

So much for business. Perhaps you may be interested in just a little personal matter. Mrs. Walker and our whole family are fairly well. We are greatly enjoying our work here at Milligan. It is a beautiful part of the country and we have a wonderful student body and faculty. If you should decide to come to America for a rest, I believe you would be pleased with this campus as headquarters. At any rate, Mrs. Walker and I would be overjoyed if you could see fit to come here and rest for as long as you feel the need of it and come and go as you like. No one will know, Earl and Ottie Mearl, how much you two have meant to Mrs. Walker and myself. We have felt too deeply to express ourselves on paper and now look forward to the time when your furlough may give us an opportunity to express personally some of the debt which we feel toward you. I have many things to say to you that I cannot say by letter. The nature of some of them you will undoubtedly surmise, but meantime we are carrying on, looking toward an expansion of the program with which you are already familiar. Our hearts go out to you with deep anxiety because of the difficulties under which you have worked, the loneliness and the bafflements which have besieged you, and the distress which you have met on every side and which has given you such anxiety. We pray, our Heavenly Father, that we shall see our way through this problem. Meantime our best love and admiration.

In considering Dr. Walker's advice, we had to take into account that it was indeed a critical time to leave the work in Germany. Students had arrived to study with Earl and at the University; children and adults were meeting regularly for services; land had been purchased for a proposed college, and Lois Lorack had arrived and was a valuable helper. Earl suggested that she oversee the work in general so that we could go on furlough. A ground floor room overlooking the Neckar River had been rented in Gartenstrasse for the meetings. Ehrfried Frank, Herr Wagner who had been recently baptized, and Gunther Brockhaus, a member of the Bruder Gemeinden, would do the preaching and Bible studies and Christa Birkholz would be in charge of the children's work. Ehrfried would also continue to study at the University. A young man, Wilfried Biering, had come into the community who would later become Lois' husband. The last Sunday before we departed on furlough, December 3, 1950, Earl baptized six people, including Wilfried. Some of the others were Heinrich Link, Christa Birkholz, and Ingeborg Proehle, a visual artist.

It was a big responsibility to leave the work in Lois' hands, but we knew of no other way to preserve what had been started. In addition to her own income from churches in the U.S., she would need funds to keep the work going. It was decided to send $150 a month to care for the meeting-room for the children's work and adult worship services, plus student expenses for studying at the University. When Lois Lorack and Wilfried Biering finally married, they rented an apartment forty-five minutes from Tübingen.

Chapter Seven
Furlough (1950–1953)

1.
Home Again! And the Birth of Vivian Jane

It was well known to friends and family that we had no place to call home in the U.S. and so we began to receive invitations from friends to stay with them even before we left Germany.

Burton Thurston, minister of Englewood Christian Church, Chicago (Earl's living link church), wrote: "We will be able to care for you and Ottie Mearl in our home here at Englewood. . . . We want you to understand that when you come to the States, the people of Englewood want to take you in and care for you and do what they can for you in the way of providing a home for you in this country. So when the occasion arises for you to return, we want you to know that there is one place that especially wants you."

Concerned about the work we were leaving behind, Dr. Walker wrote: "Mrs. Walker and I have ample room in which you may be quite at home and we can go over matters much more thoroughly and satisfactorily if we can talk and then go about our work and then come back and talk again."

Earl's father wrote: "We will have plenty of room for you and you know that it is your home too. We hope very much that you can live at 3474 Finkheiner Ct., Cincinnati 38, with us while you are on furlough. The name of the street has since been changed to Tulsa Ct. We are so thankful that things have worked out so that we can live over there, for it would be a more nearly central area for you. We hope to move the last week of November" (1950).

The first Sunday in November was their last with First Christian Church in Topeka, Kansas. A reception was held that afternoon for them with some 500 people in attendance. Earl's father took a position as vice president of the Central Trust Life Insurance Company in Cincinnati—a fortunate move, for it provided them with social security which he had not had as a minister. He was with the company three years until Earl's mother's health failed and she needed constant care.

We, together with Earl Lee, set sail for home from Cherbourg, France, on the *Queen Mary* on December 9, 1950. Comparing our trip with our initial voyage to Europe on the *John Ericksson* in 1946, we were pleasantly surprised. Little Earl Lee was an added pleasure. He took his first steps alone on the boat. It was a happy moment when we arrived at the famous central train station in Cincinnati and fell into the arms of Earl's parents, C.O. and May Stuckenbruck. A surprise lay in store for them as they had not been told that we were expecting a second child. During the next three months, they did everything they could to ease our transition back into American life. And then, on March 2, 1951, Vivian Jane was born in the Cincinnati Good Samaritan Hospital

Shortly after Jane's birth, Dr. Dean E. Walker, president of Milligan College, phoned Earl to say that the German professor at Milligan College had died. Would Earl take his place until a successor could be found? There would be housing on campus, a steady income, and the opportunity to consult with Dr. Walker about future EES work. When our little daughter was two weeks old, we moved onto the Milligan College campus.

Although Earl did teach German and eventually a course in philosophy as well, he was speaking in churches on weekends and sometimes during the week as well. Warren Mathis was able to make a 1941 Ford available for him to use in his travels close by. It was not an easy schedule and Earl felt that his performance in both areas was less than adequate.

If our two month old daughter, Jane, could have written, this would probably have been her first diary entry, telling of our arrival at Milligan College:

> Daddy decided to take a four room house on the campus. When I was two weeks old, Mother and Daddy took Earl Lee and me by plane from Cincinnati to Tri Cities Airport in Tennessee, ten miles from Johnson City. Arthur Edwards, prof. at Milligan and minister of the Hopwood Christian Church, met us at the airport and took us to his home where we had lunch. After lunch, we went to the home of President and Mrs. Dean E. Walker. At 6 p.m. Daddy came for us and we walked to our new home. He had turned on all the lights in the house and my first home was a welcome sight to my parents. All the seven years of their married life, they had lived in apartments; this was their first house for a home. Our new home was an old house with round hedges along the pathway from the front door to the street. Around the front of the house was a large, lovely lawn.

In the meantime, Paul Bajko, our Polish friend who had visited with us in Germany, had married Adela Burghardt and had completed his course of study at Eastern Christian Institute. They came to Milligan College so that he could standardize his degree and lived next door to us on campus. Earl located churches that paid Paul's tuition.

Paul had met his wife in a displaced persons camp in Germany after the war. They were married after Paul came to study at Eastern Christian Institute and she had emigrated from Germany with her parents to Canada. We were glad they could live next door to us on the Milligan College campus where we became acquainted with "Dela" as we came to call her.

Interestingly enough, it was discovered that Dr. Theodore Mosalkow, Adela's uncle, and his wife, Else, lived in Reutlingen, near Tübingen. Dela wrote her uncle to get in touch with us when we returned to Germany. In the meantime, when Earl had to be away in deputation work, Dela taught his German class at Milligan College.

After standardizing his degree at Milligan College, Paul was invited to teach at the Institute at East Orange, N.J. and to lead the newly organized Department of Missions. From their base there, he and Dela ministered to Slavic people, not only in this country, but also among their own people in Poland through the work started by evangelist Constance Jaroshavitsch. It was indeed a joy to know this fine couple. Theirs is a story of love and service to the Lord in this country and abroad.

"Cast your bread upon the water...." (Ecclesiastes 11:1) came to mind years later when Paul and Adela's daughter, Yvonne, her husband, John Marr, and their son, Tony Marr, were on the staff at First Christian Church in Johnson City, Tennessee, where we were members (and where I am still a member) and they ministered to us.

We visited our living link churches in the spring of 1951. In April of that year, we were present for a Missionary Conference at the Lock Haven, PA., Church of Christ, my living-link church, where Bill and Edythe Thompson, ministered. They had been effective public relations advocates, and the people of the church were generous supporters of the European Evangelistic Society.

While at Lock Haven, we stayed in the home of Mr. And Mrs. Hartford M. Grugan, who gave a reception so that we could meet the church people. Mrs. Anna Earon was our contact person on the missions' committee for the church. Her daughter, Mrs. Mary Jane Sarvey, wrote about the beginning of the relationship of the Lock Haven Church of Christ with the EES:

In 1948, Dr. Dean E. Walker visited the Lock Haven First Church of Christ and challenged its congregation to become a partner in an exciting new missionary project.

After having spent countless millions of dollars on two World Wars, wasn't it now time for Americans to invest money to send the New Testament Gospel to Europe? The EES, with Dr. Dean E. Walker as its president, was organized to do just that!

A young couple, Earl and Ottie Mearl Stuckenbruck, accepted a challenge to go to Europe to find a suitable place for the Mission. They finally chose Tübingen where scholars from all over the world come for advanced study in theology, as a logical place for the work of the New Testament Church.

The congregation of this church undertook a partnership with the EES at its inception and to this day remains a strong supporter of its work in Tübingen.

The Stuckenbrucks became a special missionary family to this congregation and their lives and work became intertwined with ours for many years.

In May 1951, we also participated in a Missionary Conference at Englewood Christian Church in Chicago, Earl's living-link church. Mildred (Mrs. Ben) Valiquet, a member of the church and a diligent worker among the women, had been of great encouragement to those left behind to carry on the work in Tübingen during our absence. She had rallied the ladies of the church to send parcels of food and clothing to be distributed. They also sent baptismal robes. When Lois Lorack and Wilfried Biering were married in Germany, Mrs. Valiquet sent a set of her own mother's silverware and an afghan. Following our visit to the church, Mrs. Valiquet wrote: "Your stay here was one of the highlights of our lives, and we loved having you. I am afraid we about wore you folks out as we are used to late hours. I, too, feel that the Missionary Conference was a success for those who attended. I only wish more people could have heard your message.

A lady from one of the circles came to me later and said how now she understood why we should have missionaries in Europe while before, she could not see the point."

Over a year passed. In the summer of 1952, we attended Ministers' and Missions' Week at Lake James in Indiana where the big talk was about the establishment of a graduate school of theology "somewhere." Dr. Dean E. Walker led the discussions. In addition to being president of Milligan College and the European Evangelistic Society, he had still another dream for the future of the Restoration Movement.

While Earl was doing deputation work among churches at large, I was a speaker at Ladies Aid groups and, on special occasions, in churches near Milligan College. I also participated in campus activities. Together with Florence Walker, wife of the president, we organized a Zelotai Club for wives of ministerial students and theological faculty after the pattern of the Zelotai Club on the School of Religion campus at Butler University of which both of us had been members. We drew up by-laws for the same. One of the first functions of the Zelotai Club was a *Guest Day* at Milligan College to attract area residents, which I chaired. LaVern Morse spoke and Adela Bajko had the devotions.

2.
Fund-raising

A primary responsibility of Earl while in the U.S. was the raising of funds to build on the property that had been purchased in Tübingen. Florence Walker said to me on one occasion, "I do hope Earl will be able to raise sufficient funds for the EES. Its continuance or closing depends on it." Fifty thousand dollars was the goal. There was concern all around when it became evident that insufficient funds were coming in to care for basic needs, much less the building project.

The idea of a bi-monthly paper, called the *European Evangelist*, had been conceived in 1950 for promoting the work of the EES. Copies were made available at the October 1950 International Convention in Chicago. Warren Mathis was editor. For a time, Warren also had the title of Promotional Secretary for the EES. On behalf of the nominating committee, Mathis wrote letters to Theo O. Fisher, Dougald McColl, Raymond M. Wolford, Joseph a Garshaw, Robert W. Shaw, and W. Dale Brock, inviting them to become members of the EES Board of Directors.

Rumblings of discontent in the churches increased the difficulty of raising funds. The International Convention wanted to restructure the movement. More conservative groups did not wish to go along. The resulting tension affected missions.

As a reporting agent to the International Convention of Disciples of Christ, the EES approached their Commission on Budgets and Promotional Relationships and asked to be allowed to launch a capital funds campaign among the churches. The EES, it was stated, needed funds to build a unit of the proposed theological school in the university city of Tübingen, Germany. On June 17, 1952, Earl, accompanied by Theo Fisher, minister of Northwood Christian Church, Indianapolis, and Warren Mathis, minister of Fountain Square Christian Church, Indianapolis, went before the Commission and presented the need. Gaines Cook, Executive Secretary of the International Convention of Disciples of Christ, responded in a letter to Dean E. Walker, president of the EES, June 26, 1952: "Mr. Stuckenbruck made an excellent presentation," he wrote.... "I regret to advise that the following action was taken: *Voted* that the request of the European Evangelistic Society for a Building at the University of Tübingen, Germany, be not approved."

There was a meeting of the Commission on Budgets and Promotion in Indianapolis March 2, 1953. Although Dean E. Walker missed the meeting by ten minutes, it was said that Burton

Thurston represented the EES in a fine way. One question asked in relation to establishing a seminary in Tübingen was, "Would it not be better for students to have a liberal arts education before seminary training?" Thurston explained to them the European system of education.

In April, 1953, Dean Walker informed us that he had received a letter from Gaines Cook saying that the Commission on Budgets and Promotion had now approved the EES application for the privilege of raising funds for a building in Tübingen. There was a question as to what that approval meant. Cook concluded his letter: "You have accepted a rare challenge. I pray that it will receive a response." Dale Fiers, president of the International Convention, responded favorably: "I hope somehow in the providence of God the great dreams which you have may be effectively implemented for the extension of the Kingdom of God and the glory of the Heavenly Father."

It was not easy to explain the vision for work in Europe, but an attempt was made each year in a report to the International Convention of Christian Churches. The following report by D.E. Walker was published in the Year Book, 1952.

> The European Evangelistic Society is intent upon a witness in Europe to the tradition of Jesus Christ which will accomplish a twofold objective: commend this tradition for acceptance by various segments of Christendom which have overlaid it with developments of many centuries and proclaim it for the conversion of people to unity of fellowship in Christ.
>
> We think this is a time of critical opportunity for such a witness. There are pockets of inquiry, stimulated by ecumenical intercourse, into the significance of the nature of God for the constitution of the Church. More scholars than at any time since the Reformation are subjecting the traditions of their own churches to review.

Their concern is accentuated by the growing threat of secular ideas and totalitarian forces to any form of Christianity. Despite the inclusion of nearly all the people in most countries of Western Europe within some church system by infant baptism, a mounting mass of people is apathetic to religious institutions beyond the nominal connection demanded of them.

In view of these factors we are persuaded that an academic approach is the most strategic, one which provides access to theologians with the facts and precepts of the New Testament which are of divine origin and universal validity, and one which invites students of various churches and countries to investigate these matters for eventual evangelistic service. Only a school which is adjacent to a recognized university and faculty of theology, where students can take a normal course if qualified, and which allows for distinctive teaching according to the New Testament, will suffice for this approach.

At Tübingen, Germany, a fine opportunity exists for this school. It can be built as soon as funds are available. We already own a site in this university city, and are ready with the design of an eminent local architect for construction.

Unfortunately, resources are not yet adequate. However, Mr. And Mrs. Stuckenbruck are impelled to go back to Germany at this time by the urgency of counsel with students and others who had shown an interest in our work. They cannot attempt a teaching program without facilities for this purpose, but will open further contacts with young men at various universities to interest them in the plea of Christ for the unity of His Church.

In 1954, Norman Berry was invited to become full-time Field Promotion man for the EES. He consented and was scheduled, according to correspondence, to begin June 13, 1954. His permanent address was Hutchinson, Kansas. However, there were no funds for him to begin working for the EES.

In 1955, Norvil Underwood resigned a successful pastorate in Newton, Kansas, to become a field worker for the EES. The plan was that he and his wife would travel all over the U.S. in a house trailer in behalf of the work. During his seven-year ministry at Newton, a $90,000 Religious Education building was erected and 400 were added to the membership. He served on the board of the Kansas Bible Chair at K.U. and was a member of the State Student Work Committee.

Because of their connection with Disciples Churches, Berry and Underwood were contacted and allowed to raise funds for a college in Tübingen, but there was a lack of finance to get started. Of special interest to Earl was that Underwood had taken the bedside confession of faith of his uncle, Henry Finegan, father of Jack Finegan, author of *Light from the Ancient East,* in Sioux Falls, Iowa.

3.
Considering the Future

During this time, there were many conferences with people and much talking with the Lord about how to proceed. By the end of 1952, those who were financially supporting the European effort were becoming restless. By October, 1951, the scene had changed in Tübingen and in July, 1952, everything had deteriorated. Lois's husband, Wilfried, had lost his job while funds coming from supporting churches in the States for Lois had diminished. In addition, German helpers, except for a chauffeur and an elderly lady, were gone and we had not returned to Germany. Discouraged and heartbroken because she felt that she had let the church "die,"

Lois and family (by that time David, their first child, had been born) returned to the States. This meant, of course, a disruption of the work in Tübingen.

Meanwhile, our little daughter, Jane, had been diagnosed as having a severe hearing loss, and we were having second thoughts as to the advisability of dealing with her handicap in a foreign land, that is, if we returned to Germany. We prayed earnestly for guidance. However, we could not forsake the work that had been entrusted to us since there was an open door with no one else interested in a commitment to enter it. We sensed the leading of the Lord to return to Tübingen and face the consequences as they arose. With faithful co-workers such as Dean E. Walker, Herbert Wilson, Warren Mathis, Bill Thompson, and Burton Thurston and others in the States, we were willing to launch out again.

Earl and I became convinced that unless we returned to Europe immediately, even without sufficient funding, much of the momentum for continuing the work would be lost. Earl was in contact with several young men who had expressed an interest in learning more about the objective of the EES in Europe. Among them were Iwan Petresky, a Russian in Paris; Johannes Stupp, a Hungarian studying in Germany; Fritz Schmitt in Neuss, Germany; Gunther Brockhaus in Mettmann, Ruhr Gebiet, Germany, and Ehrfried Frank who had already been related to the work in Tübingen. Unless the EES could realize the importance and, yes, the urgency of helping these young men in working for New Testament Christianity in Europe, an opportunity would be missed.

Bill Thompson wrote Earl: "Your deep devotion to the students in Germany and to the little flock at Tübingen humbles me. God bless you. Difficult as it is to return without the promise of adequate building support, I concur with you in your decision to bolster up the spirits of these young men. . . . The Missionary Committee is keeping the favorable sentiment alive."

Chapter Eight
Beginning Our Second Term in Tübingen

1.
Return to Europe and the Birth of Dale

On February 4, 1953, Earl left Johnson City to return to Europe. A local newspaper carried the news:

> Members of the Milligan College Faculty had a dinner in compliment of Prof. Earl Stuckenbruck, who is leaving this week for Germany. He is planning to continue his missionary work under the European Evangelistic Society. Professor Arthur Edwards was chairman of the evening and toastmaster.
> Commendations for Stuckenbruck's work were given by Professors Lone Sisk, Eugene Price, Ray Stahl, Frank Hannah, Sr., and President Dean E. Walker. Special music was furnished by Miss Ruth White and Prof. Warren Fairbanks.
> Stuckenbruck has been teaching at Milligan for the past year and a half. Mrs. Stuckenbruck and the children will join him in Germany later in the year.

On his way to Tübingen, Earl stopped in Paris where he became acquainted with Iwan Petresky, a Russian refugee studying at the Institut Biblique. This evangelical institution was a family affair, the teachers being the two daughters and grandson of the founder. Iwan had contact with the non-instrumental brethren in Germany but had distanced himself from them because of their restrictiveness and had gone to Paris where he was in touch with a number of other Russian refugees. From there he had written Gaines Cook and asked for help. Mr. Cook sent the letter to Earl. Realizing Petresky's potential, Earl arranged for him to register at the Free Faculty of Protestant Theology in Paris. Theological students were automatically accepted as matriculated students of the Sorbonne so that they could attend lectures in its various faculties. Incidentally, there had been no theological faculty at the Sorbonne (University of Paris) since the disestablishment of the Roman Catholic Church in about 1905. It was obvious to Earl that the Free Faculty of Protestant Theology had developed the same relation to the Sorbonne that we had envisioned between a school in Tübingen and the university

In addition to his university work, Iwan wanted to evangelize among Slavic people, first in Paris, but also among pockets of Russian refugees in Strasbourg and Munich. On February 15, 1953, Earl attended an evangelical church (Russian) with Iwan in Paris. About thirty-five people were present. The service was conducted very much like the Churches of Christ in England. There was reading of the Word of God, singing, offering, sermon, prayers of the church, and communion from a communal cup. After the benediction, men and women greeted each other respectively with the holy kiss on both cheeks. They did not include Earl, as this ceremony seemed to be reserved for members only.

While in France, Earl, in his characteristic thoroughness, explored the possibility of having a center at the University of Strasbourg. However, the university was not accepting German students because of the bitter scars left by the Nazis. He investigated Saarbrucken University but discovered that it was new and had no Faculty of Theology yet. As a result, he became more than ever convinced that Tübingen was still the right choice.

Back in Tübingen, Earl met with Artur Achstetter, the architect who had earlier drawn up plans for the seminary building. He knew of a two story home being built by Dietrich Stockmeyer, a lawyer, at Schlossbergstr. 40. For a sum of $750 or 5,000 D.M.'s up front, (a loan that would be repaid), we would be able to rent the ground floor as soon as it was completed. The EES agreed to the arrangement.

Earl learned from the Lang family, from whom we had rented living quarters when we first arrived in Germany, that Beauford Bryant, a PhD candidate at the University of Edinburgh in Scotland, was studying in Tübingen for the semester. He had gone to their home looking for a room. This was good news, and we spent many golden hours with Beauford, discussing theology and the culture and life of people in the area. He learned German well enough to preach one Sunday after services were resumed in the Gartenstrasse meeting room.

With the housing problem for the family settled, Earl took a train to Neuss where he spent a couple of days talking with Fritz Schmitt and becoming acquainted with his wife and their parents. Fritz, in spite of difficulties with the faculty of theology because of his stand on baptism, had just completed his theological exam at Muenster University. Although he had refused to have his baby "baptized," he still needed more time to study the question. He was under pressure from both his family and his wife's to conform to tradition. Earl decided it was wise to leave him to explore the Scriptures to find his answers without discussions with him. Also, since their marriage, Annaliese, Fritz's wife, had continued to live with her parents, and Fritz felt he must now assume financial responsibility for his family. He was offered a position by the Landeskirche where he would not be obliged to "baptize" infants. If he took it, he would have time to reflect on questions that would determine his future. In the meantime, Earl kept in touch with Fritz through correspondence.

Earl returned to Paris April 22nd, 1953, and found a room at Hotel Brea, 14 Rue Brea, for $1.35 a day—$40 a month. While awaiting his family's arrival, he kept fully occupied: counseling with Iwan Petresky, working on a tract for Russian speaking people, and learning French.

In the meantime, Earl still had to take care of legal matters in Tübingen from a distance. In a letter to me dated May 13, 1953, he wrote: "We need to commit our lives and this mission to the Lord more than ever so that we can fulfill His purpose in it. That is all that matters. If we cannot accomplish anything for Him, there is little use to put our lives into it. But the opportunity is before us in a wonderful way, I am sure, from the things which I see here, if we can just coordinate our efforts to that end."

He was convinced that the work should proceed with an academic approach so that the Gospel could be related to the full cultural background of the people. He was also aware that the German people are trained to respect those who are specialists in their fields and are influenced by them.

I received both encouragement and help as I waited with the children to hear from Earl that housing had been found in Tübingen. Margaret Edwards often came to bathe the children and read to them evenings while Ida Mae Kepler and I packed. Florence Walker helped with errands. A Johnson City newspaper gave an account of some of our activities before our departure.

> A tea complimenting Mrs. Earl Stuckenbruck of Milligan, who is leaving next week to join her husband in Germany, will be held Sunday afternoon at the home of Mrs. Dean E. Walker, Milligan College campus.
>
> Mrs. Stuckenbruck will be accompanied by their two children, Earl Lee, three years old, and Jane, two. Stuckenbruck left the United States for Germany about the first of the year after serving as professor of German at Milligan College for two years.

Dr. Dean E. Walker booked passage for the children and me on the *S.S. United States* for Friday noon, May 22, from Pier 86, West 46th Street, New York, and arranged for a representative at Le Havre to assist us on our way. A telegram was waiting for us on the boat: "May God sail with you and bless your return to Europe and to Earl to whom also we send our love. Signed: Florence and Dean."

When we arrived in our cabin, we were greeted by Bill and Edythe Thompson, who ministered to my living link church at Lock Haven, PA., their children, Jimmy and Bill; Mrs. Galloway and John Phelps, also a minister, who had come to say good-bye. We had a little prayer-meeting together and then they went away. Their presence and prayers were an added encouragement and provided precious memories for the future. We went out on deck. Hundreds of people were waving on the pier as our boat moved out into Hudson Bay on its way to Europe.

A letter, entitled "Pen Pictures from Europe," written October 5, 1953, under the guise of Earl Lee and Jane describes our first weeks back in Tübingen.

> Dear friends in the States,
>
> We would like to be able to draw pictures of our experiences here, but since we can't do that yet, for, you see, we are only two and three years old, we are using Mother for our secretary to send you some pen pictures from Europe.
>
> As most of you know, Daddy flew to Europe February 7 to continue the work and to find a place for us to live as a family. We hear people talking about the thousands of refugees who have crossed over the border into Western Germany and they say it is a real problem to find housing for them. Some houses are being built but not nearly enough to meet the demand. Bernd and Christel's father, Rudolph Geyer, is a builder. (They are friends in Stuttgart, Germany.) He says the German people don't have the money to do much building. Most of those who build must have some government or private loans. Anyhow, after many weeks of searching, Daddy finally found an apartment for us in Tübingen.

Four months ago, as Mother, Jane, Dr. and Mrs. Walker, and I stood at the Tri Cities Airport in Tennessee and watched Daddy fly away into the sky in an airplane, they told us that he was going to find a place for us to live and then we would all be together again. During the following weeks, I kept asking Mother if Daddy had found a place and finally one day she answered in the affirmative. I thought Daddy would come down from the sky, but he didn't come! Mother began to pack our things and to say we were going to see Daddy.

There was lots of activity at our house. Mrs. Bajko and Grace Rowe kept Jane and me most every day. Mrs. Lawrence Kepler came over and worked late at night with Mother so she could finish the packing. Dr. Walker helped Mother arrange passage by train and boat so we could see our Daddy. Then one afternoon, we got into Dr. Walker's car and he and Mrs. Walker took us to the train station in Johnson City. Aunt Margaret, Uncle Art, David, Stephen, and Phillip came to the train station to see us off. We rode on the train all night and when we awakened we were in Cincinnati where we saw Grandmother and Grandfather Stuckenbruck. The next day we got on the train and rode all night again. When we started to get off the train, Mr. and Mrs. Randall Smith and Mr. and Mrs. M.S. Kitchen were waiting for us. We were in New York City! I had never heard so much noise nor seen so many people!! They took us over to Pier #986 where I saw the big boat we were to go on. It was so huge, much bigger than our house at Milligan College. The next day, May 22nd, Mr. and Mrs. Kitchen, their daughter and Aunt Pearl took us again to the pier and we got on a big boat.

For four days and six hours we moved on the water and docked at 1:30 a.m. May 27 at Le Havre, France. There was so much noise on the ship that night that Jane and I did not sleep until about 5 a.m. While we slept, Mother went out on deck and scanned the pier for Daddy, but he was not there. Then she came back to the cabin, dressed us, and we went to the dining room at 6:30 a.m. for breakfast. When we got upstairs again, Mother and Jane and I stood in a long line to get our landing cards and let the French authorities look at our passports.

I kept wanting to know where our Daddy was but no one knew. Mother would only say he was waiting for us on the pier. We got our suitcase from the cabin and some man carried Jane down the gangplank while Mother held onto me and the luggage (a frequently used word in my vocabulary during the past few weeks). I looked at each man on the gangplank and on the pier to see if he could be my daddy, but he was not there. Then we entered a great big room and standing in the doorway of yet another room was my Daddy!! I saw him first! I was so happy!!! I didn't know whether to cry or laugh. Daddy and Mother wept a little and Jane sat on Daddy's lap and laughed and laughed. Now I knew that Daddy had found a place for us and had come down out of the sky!!! We were all together again!!!

At LeHavre we got on the boat train that took us to Paris. We talked all the way. I probably talked most of all.

In Paris we climbed three floors up a spiral staircase in Daddy's hotel to the room that would be our home for almost a week. Downstairs, Daddy talked to a French lady at a desk and nearly always his last word to her was "Merci." When I called her "Merci" Daddy and Mother laughed. I didn't understand why.

It was at Hotel Brea, our hotel, that a big man, a Russian Christian, came one day and Daddy told me that he is going to work for Jesus in Paris among the Slavic people. Iwan Petresky came many times to see Daddy and they talked about winning people for Christ. Sometimes they went out together to talk to others about Jesus and to hunt a room in which to hold services

On Sundays, we miss going to Bible School at Hopwood. Aunt Margaret was our teacher there and we think she was pretty wonderful. Now we have Bible School in our room. Daddy and Mother are our teachers. We sing all the songs we know and Daddy tells us stories from the Bible. Last night, he told us about the time Peter walked on the water to meet Jesus. I liked that one! After Daddy tells us a Bible story we always talk to Jesus and thank Him that we are together again.

June 2 we left our hotel room very early and got on another train. For twelve hours we rode until we came to Stuttgart, Germany. A big man was there to meet us with a half dozen yellow roses. Rudolph Geyer took us and our luggage in his borrowed car to Sillenbuch, a suburb of Stuttgart, where he had reserved a room for us in a small hotel near his home. Mrs. Geyer and Christel and Bernd were there. They had not gone to the Bahnhbof (station) because there would not have been room for everybody to ride in the Volkswagen, the most common of German cars.

Jane wants to tell you something now. Christal, who is eleven years old, brought her doll and its clothes which she had knitted herself. I hadn't held a doll since we left our home in Tennessee and now she let me have hers. It was so pretty! I loved it. I fed it. I washed it. I took its clothes off and put them on again several times. Christel let me keep it all night. When we went to her house for dinner the next day, Mother insisted I leave the doll there. I miss it and will be so glad when we go to our new home in Tübingen so I can see my own doll again.

The pen pictures we have given you this time are some of our experiences. We would love to receive letters from you. So do write us!

Lots of love, Earl Lee, and Jane

The middle of June, 1953, we arrived in Tübingen. Dr. Stockmayer and his children, Helmuth and Gisela, met us at the train station. The children had been taught to say our names and a few words in English. We moved into the ground-floor apartment of a new home, Schlossbergstr, 40, Tübingen, owned by the Dietrich Stockmayer family, who lived in the apartment above ours.

The ensuing nine years, without furlough, were not easy as we pioneered a unique mission, often with insufficient funds. We felt very much alone at times, except for our fellowship with the Lord. Our spiritual resources were sometimes challenged. However, our Heavenly Father stood by us even during times when we felt unworthy. Our continuing adjustment required creativeness, patience, and other attributes we didn't know we had. Nevertheless, we were convinced that we were where God wanted us to be.

A letter, written as from Earl Lee, describes our first Christmas, after returning to Tübingen, and our adjustment to life in the country we came to love:

> December 5, 1953
>
> Our dear friends in the States,
> Only twenty more days till Christmas and we're sure most of you are making preparations for a thrilling season. My parents say that the biggest thrill of Christmas is to make realistic in the lives of others and ourselves that "God so LOVED the world that He gave his only Son." (Jn. 3:16) This is one of the Bible verses they've taught us and, of course, you know the chorus, too, "For God So Loved the World." I wish we could have the fun of singing it together with you.
> Speaking of Christmas and *The* baby who was born at that time long ago, we have a surprise for you. At our house we have a little baby, too. He was born on Daddy's birthday, October 30. Both of us boys have something in common with our dad. I, of course, have his name. Jane and I think Dale is pretty wonderful!

Mechthild, the little three-month-old German baby who lives in the apartment above ours, was six weeks old when her mother and daddy had her "baptized." They didn't take her out of the house until this was done. Mechthild's Opa (grandfather) was at one time minister of the main Lutheran Church in Tübingen, and that's where her parents took her for the big event. She was dressed in her prettiest clothes and was the main attraction for all who were present at "Die Taufe," (the baptism) which included some close relatives, the midwife, Schwester Gisela, and a couple of friends. Mechthild slept through it all, except when the minister sprinkled a little water on her head. Then she drowsily opened her eyes and wondered what was happening.

We were invited to tea in the Stockmayer apartment which followed this service where coffee and cake were served. Everybody was interested in the place on Mechtild's forehead where the minister had touched her with his wet fingers. This is a big event in the life of every Christian family in Europe.

Several of the children in the neighborhood have asked when Dale is going to be "baptized." Mother tells them he will determine that when he is old enough to know what he believes and why. They always look a little disappointed for then they know they'll not be invited to the fun and tea which customarily follows such an occasion. But Jane and I invite children to visit us often. Several times we've made popcorn when they've come. It is new to them but they like it very much and always come back for more.

December 6 is the day when St. Nicholas comes in Germany. The night before, the children set their shoes outside the door and St. Nicholas leaves nuts and fruit in them. Sometimes St. Nicholas comes in the evening in person with his helper to see the children.

Dr. Stockmayer arranged through the Stiftskirche for him to visit Helmuth, Gisela, Jane, and me. About 7:30 p.m. we were ushered into the living room where we sat with expectancy as he came into full view. St. Nicholas was dressed in black with white specks of cotton on his suit to indicate he had been out in the snow. On his back he carried a sack of nuts and fruit and in his hand a bunch of switches. His helper was dressed in white and on his tall cap was a gold cross. In his hand he carried a black book and therein were written the names of all children (that's what he told us.) and the good and bad deeds they had done. He read that Helmuth had not been nice to Gisela and that he had not practiced his flute enough. Then Helmuth had to play a piece on his flute and Gisela had to sing. St. Nicholas scolded them and banged on the table in front of them with his switches. We were all a little terrified and I cried. Gisela cried, too. Jane and I had never seen a St. Nicholas like him before. He wanted to give me some nuts, but he didn't seem very kind, so I waited until he laid them down before I would take them.

On Christmas Eve, German children expect to receive more gifts. The Christmas trees are decorated with real candles. Then the children are sent out of the room. The candles are lit and the Christ Child puts gifts under the tree for all. When the children return, they sing carols and examine their unwrapped gifts.

In the room on Gartenstrasse, members of the Church of Christ and some others will be remembering the birth of Jesus on December 23. Daddy and Mother told me that they are going to use the slides concerning the birth of Jesus which the Englewood Church in Chicago sent to help in the work. Then the Mission Study Group of the Hopwood Memorial Christian Church at Milligan College and the Bierings, who used to work for Christ in Tübingen, are making it possible to give each person present a wonderful gift—a New Testament!

Through this book they can come to know, to love and work for Jesus whose birthday we celebrate. I know how much it will mean to them for I already have a New Testament.

We will be thinking about you all December 25 and wishing for you much happiness.

Thank you very much for your letters. Do write us all about *your* Christmas. Lots of love, Earl Lee.

2.
Salvaging the Work in Tübingen

We now proceeded to do what we could to salvage the work in Tübingen which was begun earlier. Worship services and Bible study were resumed. We tried to visit all of the people with whom earlier contact had been made although some of the displaced persons had moved on. Quite a few of the students had gone elsewhere to study, including Erfried Frank and his wife, Christa, who had moved to Stuttgart where Erfried worked for the U.S. Armed Forces as a supply person for a commissary. They visited Tübingen before immigrating to the U.S. in 1955, where they settled in Whittier, California.

New contacts, however, were soon made. One person, Frau Ellen Schmeißner, sought us out. Albrecht and Brigitte, her children, had participated in the Children's Hour held by Christa Birkholz and Lois Lorack. Her husband was a Methodist preacher but was not involved in a pastorate. Prof. Koeberle, who rented an apartment in the Schmeißner's home, had mentioned the family to us since they were "free church" Christians. Frau Schmeißner's visit was an encouragement to us to continue building up a base in Tübingen. Brigitte, a teenager, became the organist for worship services. Later she met and married an American soldier, Arthur

Thomas. They received their education at Milligan College in Tennessee and eventually, after we returned to the States in 1968, they moved back to Tübingen where they continued to be active in the congregation.

To become acquainted with theological scholars in Tübingen, Earl enrolled in seminars as time allowed. He attended one in which Professors Otto Michel and Otto Bauernfeind guided the translation and discussions of the *Epistles of Ignatius* from the first two decades of the second century. Another early seminar in which he participated was on baptism in the early Church and led by Dozent Dr. Georg Kretchmer, later professor of theology at the University of Munich. Still another seminar which Earl considered significant in those early years was one in which passages about Jewish sects were translated from Greek into German in Josephus' *Antiquities of the Jews* and *Wars of the Jews*, led again by Professors Otto Michel and Otto Bauernfeind. Other participants in these seminars were Otto Betz, later professor of theology at the University of Tübingen and helpful friend of the EES; Herman Waetjen, who became professor of New Testament at Pacific School of Religion and Herr Kamleiter, from the East Zone. Bauernfeind and Michel continued to work on *Wars of the Jews*, and some fifteen years later their texts, translations, and annotations were published, plus index—four volumes in all.

It is interesting to note that when Professor Bauernfeind heard about the birth of our third child, Dale, on October 30, 1953, he climbed the hill to our apartment to deliver a gift for him. His was only one of many courtesies shown us by local people at that time.

Through these endeavors to revive the work in Tübingen, we became more convinced than ever that an academic approach was appropriate in this setting. We would be working with scholars through research in original materials concerning Jesus Christ and the Church. Earl found it exciting to work with original source materials with others. In dealing with basics, there is not the sometimes heated divergence of opinions. The unity of the Church begins by going back to its origin, not up on some highly organized plane, he concluded. He contended that when one works with others on in–depth projects, there ceases to be language or cultural barriers. Theologians become simply Christian scholars seeking universal truth with other Christian scholars. Evangelism could be encouraged but in relation to Christian unity. It does not mean reducing an ecumenical witness to the least common denominator either. There must be a positive thrust of the Word of God beyond evangelism into the bastions of Roman Catholic and Protestant traditions. As much as his schedule allowed, Earl also participated in student discussion groups.

Earl spent time with Fraulein Helena Zeller translating his sermons and learning the German language. We sought out ways to mingle with the people. On Wednesdays and Fridays we went down to the market place in the city and mingled with the farmers and merchants. We invited people to our apartment where we could speak in leisure about the hope and saving grace available in Jesus Christ.

From May 1953 until May 1954, we had no transportation in Tübingen. There was no public bus service. We carried groceries up a hill to our apartment. Because we had to do all our visiting on foot, there were limitations as to time and energy. Nevertheless, we did what we could and rejoiced when we could bring hope where there was hopelessness.

Getting around without transportation, however, limited our activities. When we returned to Europe, Warren Mathis picked up the car he had made available to us while we were on furlough. He drove it to Indianapolis loaded with our personal effects to be stored in his home. Other things were stored with the Frank Oaks family at Milligan College. Warren raised $1,000 to apply on a car in Germany.

3.
Helpers and Visitors to Tübingen

In May, 1954, a refined looking lady opened the gate into our yard in Germany. I watched her come up the walkway to our apartment. The doorbell rang. She introduced herself. Adela Bajko, known to us as Dela, was her husband's niece, she said, and she had asked them (Dr. Theo and Else Mosalkow) to get in touch with us.

Dr. Theo & Else Mosalkow.

Frau Mosalkow mentioned their relationship with Iwan S. Prochanow, one of the leaders of the Evangelical Christian Movement in Russia. Her husband, Theo Mosalkow, had even taught in an Evangelical Seminary in Berlin where Prochanow was president. That was another link in our bonding. It was this man's story which had inspired us to want to serve in Europe. Earl was away at the time of Frau Mosalkow's visit, but he got in touch with her and her husband upon his return. This contact not only lifted our spirits but was the beginning of a lifelong working relationship.

Theodore Mosalkow was born May 29, 1882, in Moskow. He studied homeopathic medicine at the University of Moskow. One of his professors, a professed atheist, lay dying in a hospital, and Mosalkow visited him. The professor turned his face to the wall and confessed, "I can't stand dying as an atheist." If atheism is not worth dying for, it certainly is not worth living for, thought Mosalkow. He must use his skills and convictions as a missionary now. He studied at the Baptist Seminary in Hamburg, Germany, in 1913, in preparation to serve in the Cameroons, a German protectorate from 1884–1919. Near the end of World War I, he was conscripted to medically treat the masses of wounded soldiers. This service gave him German citizenship.

During the Lenin Revolution in 1918, Mosalkow's parents were murdered for their Christian faith. In 1919, by the Treaty of Versailles, Germany relinquished sovereignty of the Cameroons. He could no longer think of going there as a missionary and yet he could not return home. Else Louise, a native German, became his wife and assistant in his medical practice in Germany. Not content to practice medicine alone, he wanted to do more for the Lord. He taught at the Slavic Bible College in Berlin of which Iwan Prokonow was president, but the inflationary German economy forced the college to close. Mosalkow then worked with the German Tent Mission as an evangelist until Hitler closed it down. At that time he took over the ministry of a Baptist church in Munich. For a time during World War I, he helped care for the wounded in the U.S. Armed Forces.

Frau Mosalkow continued to care for her parents in the East Zone as long as they lived. From time to time, she crossed the border between the East and West zones to see her husband and to carry out his library and other treasures in a knapsack on her back. More than once, she was apprehended and punished with work at the "watch post," scrubbing floors and washing windows, before they let her go. Then one dark, rainy night, after the death of both parents, with oxen pulling a wagon loaded with furniture, linens, and other household items, she crossed no-man's land to freedom in the West. Shots were fired in her direction, penetrating the furniture, but she was unhurt. She soon had a new covering put on the overstuffed sofa and chairs, and they continued to be her prized possessions until her death in March, 1988.

Unable to resume tent evangelism, the Mosalkows came in 1952 to live in Reutlingen, about ten miles from Tübingen, and later in Wannweil, half way between Reutlingen and Tübingen, where they built a home with reparation funds. From there, Dr. Mosalkow began to evangelize both German and Slavic people streaming out of Communist dominated Eastern Europe. Upon making our acquaintance, he threw his energies into the evangelistic work of the EES. Eventually, the Boones Creek Christian Church in Tennessee (Art Edwards, pastor) and First Christian Church (T.K. Smith, pastor) Columbus, Indiana, took them on as living-links with a salary of $125 (500 D.M.s) a month, supplemented by a small pension from the Baptist Tent Mission. Dr. Mosalkow wrote a statement for the EES after they decided to work in evangelism with us:

>After twenty years as an evangelist with the German Tent Mission, I welcome the opportunity to work with the European Evangelistic Society for two reasons: One, so that my wife and I can devote our service to the Church of Christ which corresponds to the Evangelical Christian Movement in Russia. I began my ministry with Mr. Prokhanoff, the leader of this movement, and was associated with him in the Bible School which he conducted in Berlin for two years after the First World War. Second, so that I can reach more of my own people in Western Germany for Jesus Christ.
>
>As well as we can estimate, there are about 120,000 Slavic Displaced Persons in Western Germany. Almost no one troubles himself about their spiritual status. A few priests of the Orthodox Church come occasionally to the larger camps and hold a liturgical service. A protestant agency, Light of the East, is still active in distributing religious literature and relief supplies, but it does not attempt a positive witness of the Gospel. The Baptist World Alliance keeps up contact with Baptist people.

Except for a few larger camps, these people are scattered in smaller groups throughout the country. I have begun a combined visitation and preaching witness among them. Now, more invitations are pouring in than I can fill, especially as friends and families write each other of my visits. In view of these pleas I cannot restrict myself to a few places, but must travel extensively. By summer I hope to hold a four-week course with several of these brethren who have agreed to help their own people with me.

For a time, the church will consist of scattered members. The next step will be to evangelize at strategic points where they can form a church with German people. Eventually these Russian people who remain in Germany—and most of those who are still here will remain—will be absorbed into the German culture. Therefore we must plan for a combined Russian-German evangelistic work.

I cannot say how much it would mean to have a small tent for our evangelistic work—not because of my experience in tent evangelism. But the fact is, a tent provides the one sure neutral opportunity to invite people to hear the Gospel. It is most difficult to arrange for adequate evangelistic facilities outside of the regular churches. People who would never go to a church will come to the tent. I wish that I could lay this need upon the heart of someone or of some church until it could be realized while the opportunity is at hand.

From exiles of Russians in Western Europe we have established contact with a few churches of Evangelical Christians—in Ulm, Farel, and Berlin. But among the Displaced Persons from the Second World War few Evangelical Christians remain. Most of them have emigrated. But the hearts of others are open to the Gospel. The hardest thing for me is to break away from people after a few days of talking and visiting. When the Word of God comes into their hearts they burn within. Pray with us, that it will turn them to the living God and to his Son, Jesus Christ, our Lord.— Theodore Mosalkow, Wannweil, Germany, February, 1956.

In the meantime, Earl kept in touch with Fritz Schmitt and Iwan Petresky. Fritz accepted a tentative position with the

Landeskirche in Konken, Pfalz, so that his wife, Anneliese, could join him in their own home for the first time which would enable them to discuss important questions together. Fritz came to the conclusion that he could not conscientiously continue in the ministry of the Landeskirche. In March, 1954, Annaliese and their little daughter came to Tübingen and were our guests for a week to learn more about the Christian Church and the work of the EES on the continent. She returned home convinced with Fritz that they should consent to merging their evangelistic efforts with ours in Tübingen. In July, a second daughter was born to them. Fritz's concern was that he would be obliged to "baptize" his own daughter if they remained in his position as pastor of a Lutheran Church.

Relatives and friends questioned the decision of the Schmitts. However, the young couple seemed eager to devote their lives to the pioneer ministry in Europe with the EES. Having worked through the questions concerning infant baptism and the Lord's Supper, they were ready to put into practice their convictions. And so Earl baptized Fritz.

On March 1, 1955, an apartment was finally found for the Schmitts in Kusterdingen, a "Dorf" (a little town) seven miles from Tübingen, so that they could join their efforts with ours. At the same time as their arrival in the city, we were told by a German friend that a new pastor had come to a Lutheran Church in Tübingen. He is a "Born-again-Christian," a believer, she said enthusiastically. I asked no questions but did a lot of reflecting.

Earl and Fritz began to work together. They visited people in their homes. They went together to several out-of-town meetings. Frau Anna Steudel invited them to one such meeting in Koenigsfeld where the people wanted to know more about the Lord's Supper.

Fritz was diligent in his work. His sermons were well prepared and his Bible studies with an intermediate youth group showed creativity and held the young people's attention.

Two churches in the States became the living link support for the Schmitts: the Broadway Church in Wichita, Kansas, (Ting

Champie, minister), and Bethesda Christian Church in Washington, D.C., (Robert Shaw, minister). They wished to supplement the pledge for the Schmitts from Wauchula, Florida Church (Kenneth Bain, minister). Robert Shaw wrote:

> This assumption of so large a commitment toward one missionary project means a great deal to this congregation and to the future of its missionary commitment. I think that the feeling they were one-half responsible for the support of a particular man on a mission field was the thing that captured them to undertake such a commitment. I hope there will be nothing to occasion any doubt on their part that the action was wisely taken. It is good to know of the work as it progresses there.
>
> We are personally quite pleased at every opportunity to communicate with you and to share in the work which has been undertaken there. We have had a great personal interest in it from the very beginning both from our personal acquaintance with you and a sense of the need for such a mission in Central Europe. I think this sense of need for such a work in Europe is heightened in the Washington, D.C. area by the rather continual contact which is had here with persons from Europe and by Americans who are returning from a stay in Europe.

Unfortunately, because of the distance from Kusterdingen to Tübingen where the Schmitts had an apartment, plus the responsibility of two young children and another one on the way, Annaliese was unable to be involved in the work. With frustrations of mind and soul, she found it difficult to adjust to a new way of life which was frowned upon by her parents. To add to their problems, the family had no means of transportation except the moped which Fritz used to get around.

Iwan Petresky, however, continued to keep in touch with Earl. When our friends, Burton Thurston and Loren Fisher, stopped in

Paris on their return trip from Jerusalem to the States, they were interested in meeting Iwan and other Russian contacts and so they invited Earl to meet them there. George Fisher, a U.S. chaplain stationed at Mannheim, drove Earl to Paris where they met Thurston and Fisher.

On August 18, 1954, Iwan arranged a meeting with his Russian acquaintances and Burton spoke to them while Petresky interpreted. Some twenty Russian people had come together for this meeting. Earl had completed a tract which Petresky had translated into Russian and which was being distributed among his people in Paris and also in Strasbourg. (Johannes Stupp eventually had this tract translated into "Lettische" (Latvian) for his work among exiled students at Bad-Godesberg.)

After one semester of study and work in Paris, Petresky decided that it would be more advantageous for him to study at the Faculty of Theology in Strasbourg and that evangelistic efforts there would be more productive. He would be close enough to Tübingen for more frequent consultation and visits with Earl, while keeping in touch with his contacts in Paris. However, he was finding it difficult to have a Christian Church among his people in Paris without adequate help in reaching the unreached. It might have been possible to bring some who were already Christians together, but that tactic did not appeal to him.

In 1956, Jessie Bader, founder and general secretary of the World Convention of Churches of Christ, visited us in Tübingen. Since he was a friend and classmate of Earl's father, C.O. Stuckenbruck, an affinity was already in place. Also, in 1938–39, when Earl was president of the Student Christian Federation at the University of Kansas, he had arranged for the University Christian Mission to be on campus for four days. Jessie Bader organized the University Christian Mission and scheduled teams to visit campuses across the country. He sought out outstanding evangelists of the day for these missions, including E. Stanley Jones, T.Z. Koo, Grace Sloane Overton, Harry Cotton and Edwin

McNeil Poteat. E. Stanley Jones and T.Z. Koo spoke for two all-university convocations at K.U. to packed audiences. Earl worked with Bader, an evangelist at heart, on the project.

Having cooperated in the past so successfully with Jessie, we shared with him during his visit to Tübingen, the concern of some who felt that to evangelize on the continent was an intrusion. Bader's words of encouragement confirmed our own conviction. "If you are evangelizing, you are not intruding," he assured us. We were reminded of Prof. Adolph Koeberle's statement when we first went to Tübingen. "If we were to work night and day, we could not win ALL for Christ. We welcome your coming." In Bader's mind, evangelism superseded Christian unity. Unity that does not lead to evangelism is not real unity. In addition, evangelism that does not lead to "Christian unity is not real evangelism," he contended.

4.
Tour to the Holy Land

Further friendships were cemented through Earl's joining a study-guided tour to the Holy Land planned by YMCA personnel. In May, 1955, Earl consulted with Dr. Walker about absenting himself from Tübingen for five weeks to go with Professor Dr. Otto Michel and a group of about twenty-five theologians to Palestine. The cost would be about $300.00 and we would personally take care of these expenses. Prof. Otto Michel would be the guide at the historical sites. Earl's going was approved, and in September, the group traveled by land and sea to the Holy Land. Fritz Schmitt would remain in charge of the work in Tübingen until Earl returned.

Having just completed a three-week tour of the Near East, Prof. Michel met the group in Beirut and accompanied them the rest of the way. Sharing in this experience was not only a learning and challenging event; it enabled Earl to forge new ties with

German theologians. Otteinrich Knoedler, son of a Tübingen Lutheran pastor, was among those who went on the trip. He wrote his parents to look after Earl's family while he was away. As a result, we were invited to his home for tea. Otto Betz, Earl, and three others went on into Egypt and back up through Italy. Betz both authored and directed a drama about the Dead Sea Scrolls and presented it at the Gartenstrasse Room for the Christliche Gemeinde (Christian Church) when he returned to Germany. The group of actors included his future wife, a theological student who had been on the trip and who played the lead role!

The group met in our apartment to compare notes and exchange information. Earl created a process by which to duplicate slides before it was possible to do it in the local shops, thereby making possible the swapping of slides within the group. The YMCA used five or six of the slides for commercial purposes. Much goodwill was thus generated for our work as a result of Earl's having gone on the tour.

5.
Temporary Setbacks.

Although the work in Tübingen was progressing, there were negative voices raised against it in the U.S. A person, who worked with Church World Service in Europe following WW II, openly objected to the work of the EES in Germany at the Virginia State Convention in Norfolk and at meetings around the country in 1954. To represent our movement in Europe was to play the role of one of a number of small, disrupting sects, he contended. He had never been to Germany except for a flying trip across the border. His criticism caused a theological student of the Restoration Movement who had studied in Tübingen to ask how anyone could assess the situation who did not know the culture, the changing scene because of the influx of refugees, and the frustration of people trying to find their way in the aftermath of WW II.

Finally, this person, accompanied by a member of the Association for the Promotion of Christian Unity, decided to go to Tübingen to evaluate the work of the EES. They visited with us in our home. We were quite open in our explanation of what we were doing: evangelistic work, our contacts with students, work among refugees and Slavic people, and our dream for a Bible college or institute. They also spoke with one of the professors at the university who did not know us personally. On the other hand, U.S. military chaplains in Germany were helpful and positive in their appraisal of the presence of the EES in Germany.

Meanwhile, we were faced with disappointing news. While Earl was on the study-guided tour of the Holy Land, Fritz Schmitt had been in touch with Lutheran pastors in Baden-Wuertemberg. He wanted to be financially secure for his wife's sake. Fringe benefits for families of pastors in the traditional churches and the persuasion of family members were influential in turning the Schmitts back to the Lutheran "fold." In addition to all this, Fritz was suffering from ulcers and was ordered by his doctor to curtail his activities for a month.

When Earl went out to see the Mosalkows after the trip, Theo met him a half block away, running towards him with the news that Fritz was neglecting his work in Tübingen. He was totally unaware of Fritz's health problems and frustrations. The Mosalkows were shocked that a German with such a commitment should back down, and again and again they apologized for the action of a fellow countryman. Shortly thereafter, Fritz submitted his resignation. Earl visited Fritz and Annaliese, but their minds were made up. They told him that they felt they could keep their convictions and still minister within the Lutheran Church. Earl could only wish them well and thank God for any positive influence they had had during their Tübingen ministry. This turn of events came as a great disappointment, however, not only to us and the Mosalkows, but also to Robert Shaw, Ting Champie, and Kenneth Bain, ministers whose churches in the States had pledged financial and prayer support for the Schmitt family.

Chapter Nine
The Work Progresses

1.
The Christliche Gemeinde

In the fall of 1955, a group from the Christliche Gemeinde began to invite interested friends to their homes for a weekly Bible study. It was an opportunity to talk with them in an informal setting about a relationship with Christ and His Church. As a result, new people came to services on Sundays. A Christmas pageant, which I directed, was the highlight of the season. On the evening it was given, the walls seemed to bulge in the little room and let over sixty people crowd in. Those acting in the pageant were so thrilled, they all wanted to give it again, and their wish came true: they were invited to present it to a non-church organization.

There was a friendly atmosphere in our church. At the Sunday morning services, nobody left the church room without getting acquainted with everyone in attendance. Often foreigners were present. Earl preached, along with Mosalkow, when he was in town. Like many nationalities, most Germans do not like to adjust to a foreign nation's culture and customs. It was important, therefore, that German customs be observed. For example, many German Christians would never serve grape juice, only wine, for communion. And so at communion time, it was decided to place grape juice in the center of the communion tray and wine in cups on the outer edge to accommodate the preference of all.

The discussions during our Bible study on Wednesday evenings were interesting and meaningful, and it was difficult to part when it was over. Although Earl was equally at home with scholars and people in the market place, he was amazed at the insight of some whose formal education had been neglected. Herr Gustav Neumann was a case in point. An elderly gentleman, whose schooling had stopped after fourth grade and who had served in an African War where he lost an arm, was well-read and could pull out a Bible verse for every need. When he spoke, people listened. He was one who set the spiritual tone at prayer-meetings and Bible studies when others were satisfied to pass off questions lightly or consider them superfluous. For Earl, Herr Neuman's insights into Scripture were as valid as those of his scholarly friends. Although at home with the original biblical languages himself, still he felt that all Christians are on the same level spiritually and can learn from one another.

I was also kept busy and conducted a children's Bible class for five and six-year-olds. Friday afternoons there was another children's Bible class of nine to fourteen-year-olds that Earl led, and then on Friday nights, he met with a group of men for Bible study. The first week of every month a women's group met. Much of the activity one year was spent sewing and fixing clothing to send to the Dr. John and Mabel Ross mission in the Congo. A meaningful Bible theme for the ladies was, "Let your light so shine before men that they may see your good works and glorify your Father who is in heaven." Each semester, Earl found time to participate in seminars at the University and to counsel and pray with students who sought him out.

Hilde Cribbs, a German widow with three children, and I had started a Kinderstunde (Children's Hour) Wednesday afternoons. Soon other children joined ours for Bible stories and the singing of Christian choruses. Marlise Kost (Gellert), Maria Reinhardt (Milligan) and Gerda Kress (Schauer), three teenage German girls, were helpers. Eventually, Gisela and Dietmar Luik and many others joined this group. The Luik children received permission from the semi-private Waldorfschule they attended to allow this to be accepted as their religious instruction, religion being a required course in the school curriculum. Years later, Dina Luik and Pauline Reinhardt were teachers in the program and our daughter, Jane, was a helper.

Frau Luik used original materials for teaching the children. She received commendation from a professor of systematic theology at the University of Tübingen for the unique way in which the classes were conducted and for the materials she used. First, she told a Bible story to the children and then used creative ways to let it relate to life. Sometimes the children were asked to draw pictures to illustrate the story; at other times, they would act out the story in an original drama.

2.
Dr. Theo Mosalkow

In the fall of 1957, Earl and Dr. Mosalkow met with John Bolton in Neurnberg. He was owner of the International Standex Corporation of which Standard Publishing Company was a division. He was interested in reaching university students for Christ and had funded a European Retreat Center for the Intervarsity Movement.

Years before, John's fiancée had been impressed with Ludwig von Gerdtell and his message when he was lecturing on the Marburg University campus. She invited John to go with her to hear him and he was equally impressed. Both were already "believers." Bolton was an immersed member of the Freie Evangelische Gemeinde. John Bolton told Earl that they had liked von Gertell so well that they asked him to perform their wedding ceremony

The purpose of Earl and Mosalkow's meeting with Bolton was to invite his participation in the Tübingen European Christian adventure by supplying Dr. Mosalkow with a tent for evangelistic meetings. As an esteemed and experienced evangelist with the German Evangelical Tent Mission for more than three decades, Mosalkow had been able to reach thousands with the Gospel and was instrumental in starting a number of "free" churches. Yet Bolton was not inclined to take the "risk." In addition, funds coming from churches in the U.S. were insufficient to purchase a tent for the veteran evangelist. He decided, however, to continue his work, even though limited in his outreach.

Dr. Mosalkow was instrumental in starting three churches in northern Germany in 1954. There was great rejoicing. Tragically, however, there was no one we could suggest to them as a possible leader or pastor, and they were too young in the faith to stand alone. Earl and Theo considered a limited correspondence teaching program for young men in order to meet the emergency, but, alas, no funds were available even for that. However, one can only imagine the influence these Christians exerted, each in his individual sphere.

Mosalkow was a great help to us in establishing the Christliche Gemeinde in Tübingen. Frau Mosalkow helped with the women's work of the church. He often preached for the congregation and both were very much loved and respected. They were our Sunday dinner guests whenever he was not traveling. It was an opportunity to discuss and plan for the work. Our children claimed them as their local grandparents. Our youngest son, Loren Theo, was named after Dr. Mosalkow at the suggestion of Frau Mosalkow.

3.
Work among the Russians

Theo Moskalow and Earl went to Strasbourg and Baden-Baden to help Iwan Petresky in his evangelistic efforts. The Russian group in Strasbourg was better informed about politics than Christianity. Once when Earl tried to preach there with Petresky as interpreter, the people kept interrupting with political questions. Earl reminded them that he was there to talk about the Savior of the world who could make more of a difference in their lives than political leaders! They were a depressed group of people—confused, frustrated, and without hope—yet they refused to listen and to be guided.

On a Sunday afternoon, Earl baptized a lady, on the recommendation of Petresky, in a body of water beside the Rhine River. When pedestrians in the area saw what was happening, they gathered and voiced their disbelief, shaking their fists in disgust. The refined lady who was being baptized simply lifted her hands to heaven and praised the Lord.

There were quite a number of Russian children in Strasbourg. French children were discouraged to play with them and they were excluded from activities in the schools. Petresky started a Bible class for them. However, discouraged by the response among Russian people in general in Strasbourg, he sought out Russians in Baden-Baden.

Mosalkow and Earl sensed in Petresky a desire to oversee work among his people rather than making plans and doing the basic work of evangelizing. Petresky thought that if he could have someone working in Paris, Strasbourg, Baden-Baden, and Munich, he could oversee the work and people would be won for the Lord. To plant, water, and help a church to grow didn't seem to be something he could or wanted to do. Funds were scarce and results of his efforts were not forthcoming. Eventually, Earl had to let him find his own way through the maze of many different interests.

At Easter time, 1954, Mosalkow held a meeting for a Russian church in Brussels. At the same time he met with a nucleus of Germans. Several confessed Christ and they asked him back to baptize them on Pentecost. At age sixty-two, Dr. Mosalkow was in good health and wishing he had a second life to give in service for the Lord. His love of the Lord was contagious wherever he went. He held an evangelistic meeting in the rented room in Tübingen for a week where seventy-eighty people would crowd in each night. Two people committed their lives to Christ and were baptized.

4.
Jane and Earl Lee

At the same time that the work was progressing, Jane's hearing impairment continued to be of great concern. On the recommendation of Prof. Schwarz, head of the Ohren Klinik in Tübingen, we took her to the famous Ohren Klinik in Basel, Switzerland, where she underwent a thorough examination. The prognosis was not good. The examining physician told us that the best thing we could do for her would be to place her in a home for the deaf where she could learn to care for her needs and to communicate with her "kind."

Distraught with the idea of being separated from Jane but wanting to do the thing that would be most beneficial for her, we visited several "homes" for the deaf in Germany. Upon seeing Jane, those conducting the interviews told us, "She is too good for us," meaning she was able to receive a normal education. And so we took her home and praised the Lord that there was hope.

In a parents' magazine, passed on to us by Chaplain and Mrs. Carl Ledbetter who were stationed in Stuttgart with the U.S. Army, we found an advertisement of the John Tracy Clinic's correspondence course for the deaf. We wrote for materials and I began to teach Jane. Much repetition was needed as she learned to pronounce consonants and increase her vocabulary while she translated her mumbling sounds into intelligible speech. A speech therapist at the local Ohren Klinik, Ingeborg Weisert, began to teach Jane lip-reading in both German and English.

Eager to learn whatever she was taught, Jane made steady progress, so much so that at five she, together with Earl Lee, began to learn to play the recorder from Lisel Hartman, a young neighbor. Earl Lee was always protective of her. When we enrolled her in a German Kindergarten, he would meet Jane there every day and accompany her home. On one occasion, they saw a man hiding behind some bushes. Earl Lee grabbed Jane's hand and led her towards home through the castle at the end of our street.

Meanwhile, since they were late, we became concerned and called the police who found them and brought them safely home.

Earl Lee's protective nature helped him save each of his siblings from what would probably have been a fatal accident. Once, while I was cleaning the Gemeinde room, the children wandered down to the Neckar River. Dale reached out to retrieve a ball which had fallen into the river and fell in himself. As he was about to go under, Earl Lee caught hold of him and dragged him to shore. On another occasion, we were visiting Heigerloch. While taking a walk with the children, three-years-old Loren wandered away from us. Earl Lee found him looking down into a deep gravel pit. He gently pulled Loren away from the pit and brought him back to his anxious parents.

At age seven, Jane attended a German school. Although she did her work well and quickly, her teacher suggested that school work in higher grades would be too difficult for her to handle. Since she was an American citizen, her opinion was that she ought to be schooled in her native tongue.

For her second school year, I drove Jane to an American military school in Boeblingen, some thirty miles away, where I did substitute teaching. However, not finding it easy to be away from home and the other children during the day, I found it better to employ local teachers for Jane's instruction. Mrs. Robert (Sonia) Albers and Mrs. Robert (Janet) Jewett, whose husbands were American scholarship graduate students at the University of Tübingen and themselves certified teachers, taught her. Both were musicians, Janet having sung in the motets Saturday evenings in the Stiftskirche, so this made it possible for music to become an added dimension of Jane's instruction. Cilla Ludbrook, an Australian who volunteered her services as secretary for Earl, also helped me teach Jane during those early years. In addition, I incorporated the Calvert School Correspondence Course provided by the University of Maryland as a part of Jane's education. These lessons were simple and easy to follow.

Chapter Ten
Other Aspects of the Work

1.
Foreign Professors, Graduate Students, and Fulbright Scholars

American professors on sabbatical leave and other foreign graduate students were beginning to arrive in Tübingen to hone their particular areas of study, and the University Auslandsamt (the international office) approached Earl about helping to secure housing for them. This became an ever increasing job throughout the years. Although this was time-consuming, Earl was more than recompensed through lasting friendships formed with scholars throughout the States and other parts of the world. Many of them participated in the work of the European Evangelistic Society and broadened our contacts among German scholars.

Many stories can be told about our experiences with foreign students/professors. A couple of times, Earl drove with several of them to Basel, Switzerland, to seminars in the home of Karl Barth when someone from Tübingen was presenting a paper. The room was

Karl Barth & students in his home.

small where they met and some sat on the floor. On one occasion, I was invited to go along. One of the students, Larry Holland, spoke up:

"It has been said that you have stated that the most profound thing about the Christian faith is 'Jesus loves me this I know,'" he commented. "Is that true?"

"Yes," Barth replied, and then began to expound on the subject for a while.

In 1955, a number of Fulbright scholars arrived in Tübingen with their families. In addition to searching for housing for them, Earl was their contact person for nearly everything else. They had endless questions as they tried to adjust to life in a foreign land. Earl's hours began to stretch out of control as he sought to help them in addition to his own work. We tried to think of a solution.

I invited the wives of some of these foreign scholars to our apartment in groups to discuss their problems. It occurred to us that in this conservative area of Germany, foreigners needed some way to meet with the local residents. And so instead of trying to handle their questions alone, I invited some German ladies to come together with the Americans. This opened up contacts which would serve a worthy cause. Prior to this, many American wives had felt isolated and unhappy. Their husbands were mingling with their peers at the university while they sat at home, eagerly awaiting trips around Europe and the time when they would be able to return to the U.S. They missed out on the advantages of learning to know German families and the cultural exchange this involved.

It was indeed a strange land for newcomers. Most people lived in rather small apartments where there was little elbow room and an abundance of neighbors' nerves. It was necessary to keep the noise level low and to understand the people and try to conform to their way of life. Hilde Achstetter and I compiled information in a pamphlet for Americans and other foreigners to help facilitate the adjustment process.

2.
The German-American Women's Club

Around 1955, a German-American Woman's Club was started in Tübingen. Its founders were Dora Reich, Hilda Achstetter, and I—the three of us being united by the one desire to help foreign wives adjust to German culture.

Frau Dora Reich had lived in the U.S. at one time when her husband was a graduate medical school student. Now, back in Germany, she was keen to meet American ladies, knowing how they must feel in a foreign country. Frau Hilde Achstetter, wife of the architect who had drawn up plans for the EES college building when we first arrived in Tübingen, was grateful for the help her family had received from Americans following the war and wanted to express her gratitude by helping newcomers.

For a year or two, the three of us simply got together a group of American and German ladies for coffee in the afternoons and for a Thanksgiving Dinner in an ante room of a restaurant in the city. It was a carry-in meal to which Americans invited German friends and acquaintances.

On one occasion, when the German-American Women's Club was meeting at Frau Achstetter's home, discussions got out of hand. It was difficult to imagine that ladies exchanging ideas could be so disorderly. I was shocked. At the next meeting I presented to the club a set of rules (by-laws). The German ladies were amazed that Americans could come up with something that smelled of "order." This was especially true of a lawyer who had been responsible for most of the chaos at the previous meeting.

The ladies were glad, however, to adopt the rules. Succeeding meetings were happier and more orderly. Florence Walker would have smiled had she known that the by-laws she and I had drawn up for the Zelotai Club on the Milligan College campus served as a pattern for those drawn up for a German-American Club in Tübingen!

Again and again, foreigners expressed appreciation for the helpfulness of the German-American Club. Dr. Robert Evans, University of PA, Philadelphia, College of Religious Thought, wrote: "Thank you for giving such steady and imaginative leadership this year. I know the various activities of the club have been of value and important to many of us."

As more Americans kept coming each year and the membership increased, the club was divided into interest groups: music, literature, crafts, language, and culinary arts. Occasionally, all would come together for a special program. In this way, more intimate relationships could be formed and nurtured.

Hilde Achstetter and I went to both city and university officials and talked with them about the importance of a welcome for incoming scholars and students each year. As a result, they offered their cooperation. From that time on, we and our husbands were invited to university and city receptions where we encouraged international relationships. On one occasion, when Dr. Dean E. Walker was visiting us, we arranged for him to accompany us to one of the large receptions held at the City Hall.

Dr. Ottmar Kuhn recorded a welcome dinner for incoming American scholars in the local *Schwaebisches Tagblatt* newspaper:

> The German-American Women's Club, which since its beginning, has met in private homes, received public attention when it sponsored a Schwabian dinner of sour Kraut and Wurst for the new incoming Americans. It was financed by city, county, University, and German-American Institute funds. Wuerttemberg-Hohenzollern President Birn, Mayor Döge, Rector Prof. Dr. Gottfried Mollenstedt of the University, Dr. Rolf Fritz and Commandant Welschinger from the German-French Club and many German and American couples were present for the occasion.
>
> The Government President indicated that the G.A. Club exists in order to help Americans in their adjustment upon

arrival in Tübingen and to give them the right perspective of Germany upon their return home. Mayor Döge mentioned that Tübingen with its famous University is an intellectual metropolitan center and that its "partner-shaft" with Ann Arbor, USA, is an important cementing relationship. Prof. Mollenstedt, in his welcome address, spoke of his experiences with American people. Lenore Dahn-Wehrung, Flutist, and her husband, Karl-Heinrich Dahn, pianist, entertained the group with several musical numbers. Mrs. Ottie Mearl Stuckenbruck, co-president with Frau Hilde Achstetter of the Club, thanked the officials in the name of all Americans present. We can learn to know and understand a country and its people best through direct contact, she said, and we would count it our greatest success to know that our efforts are helping to create a better "People-to-People" relationship in the world.

Not only were foreigners helped through the German-American Club, but its outreach into the community created an acceptance of the work of the European Evangelistic Society.

Acceptance on the part of some local people was also promoted through the meeting of the World Council of Churches in New Delhi, attended by some of the church leaders in Tübingen. This meeting helped to break down denominational barriers.

3.
German Customs

Most American ladies were fascinated with German customs. If ladies were invited to a private German home, they could consider it a special gesture of friendship. The hostess carefully prepared for the visit: the house was spic and span; Kuchen was baked or bought and served with whipped cream for the coffee hour. The hostess family dressed up for the occasion. Guests took cut flowers to the hostess, usually an uneven number. They removed paper from the flowers before they presented them. The hostess did not expect a thank-you note, although she appreciated a phone call the next day. One usually greeted another with a handshake. There was protocol to this also. The lady offered her hand first to the gentleman. Little girls made a curtsy when greeting an adult, and little boys bowed while shaking hands. First names were not used upon first meeting and it always seemed to me that "Frau Schauer" did not sound as formal as its English equivalent. Then there was the ticklish business of "Sie" and "Du." "Sie" (German for the English word "you") was used for strangers and acquaintances while "du" was reserved for family, children, and close friends. Americans were not to use "du" unless expressly invited to do so, usually by the older person. Incidentally, God is addressed as "Du" as He is our Father and we belong to His family.

Unmarried women over forty had the right to be called "Frau." Married women were addressed by their own first names—e.g. Frau Gerda Schauer, not Frau Thomas Schauer. Wedding rings are worn on the right hand. Couples had a civil ceremony for weddings even although they may have already had a church wedding. Men usually preceded women when entering any public place to "check it out" first to see if it was fit for a lady to enter. The man walked on the left side of a woman in the streets.

In the 1950s, there was a specialty shop for nearly everything, and you had to know where to go for what you needed. Upon entering a store, it was polite to say "Guten Tag," and upon exiting, "Auf wiedersehen."

Germany has many holidays, and it was frowned on to have the wash hanging out on those days. Of course, not only did the newcomers have to learn to count German currency, but to know the entire metric system as well: centigrade, kilometers, and grams. It was important to have a conversion table handy while working in the kitchen or when buying clothes. Imagine giving the weight of a new born baby in grams! We were shocked when we were told that our first child, Earl Lee, *weighed 3,799 grams*!!

The first day of school for little tots was made easier and more fun by receiving a large cone filled with sweets or maybe even a toy. There were no water fountains in the schools and no lunches served. Pretzels were sold during recess in some of the schools. Most schools let out at 1 or 2 p.m.

There were to be no playing of musical instruments in apartments, no running of water for baths, and no phone calls after 9 p.m. and also between 1 and 3 in the afternoons. Soft-soled shoes were to be worn at home.

Professional people were usually addressed by their titles: e.g. Herr Professor, and sometimes his wife was "Frau Professor," although this is not the preferred custom now. One was not expected to tip anybody, except the Portier (porter), because the tips are included in the service charge. German people have a keen sense of order. There was no litter in the streets. The homes were kept clean. The floors, especially, were polished until they literally shone. You could go into the city with a button off your coat, a shoe lace untied, or a dusty spot on your clothes, and several people might draw your attention to this flaw in your attire. An American of our acquaintance was walking along the street one cold day with part of his overcoat collar turned up. A little lady he had never seen before politely approached him and told him about it. Then she reached up and put it in order, and both went on their way.

We also discovered that the Germans are, in general, well-disciplined and energetic. There was correct deportment on the part of everybody except, perhaps, the motorists. Tübingen has many narrow, winding streets, and it has been said that if one can learn to drive there, he or she could drive anywhere in the world. Driving in our town, therefore, was one of the best disciplines for the temper and nerves. Germans had a little head-tapping sign by which one motorist deliberately insulted and infuriated another. It became a punishable offense, but there were too many offenders to punish anyone. If a German motorist knew he had the right of way, he would take it even if that meant an accident. Of course, there were exceptions, or there would have been few survivors. An interesting footnote: once someone obtained a driver's license, it was good for life!

4.
Empathy With Those Who Were Seeking A Meaningful Life With Jesus

During our years in Germany, we struggled with those who had decided to become not the "only Christians," but "Christians only." Breaking with tradition in order to embrace new truth was not always easy. Even so, we did *not* insist that those seeking to obey Christ should "leave" the church with which they were affiliated.

One of the groups meeting in Tübingen was made up of "pietistic" Christians. These folks were not satisfied with the formal traditions of the Landeskirche (the Lutheran Church), and wanted to practice a more vital, personal faith. And so they clustered together in groups and emphasized conversion by the Holy Spirit and the Second Coming of Christ. Some of these people, however, did consent to immersion and even desired the Lord's Supper on a weekly basis while remaining within the Landeskirche which provided fringe benefits—an "honorable" burial, confirmation and marriage festivals, and access to health resorts at little or no cost.

5.
The work in Belgium

Dr. Deelstra, a Dutchman working as an evangelist in Genk, Belgium, contacted Dr. Mosalkow and asked if he knew of a

German who might help in his work. He had started a church and a school twenty years earlier, the only Protestant work in the predominately Roman Catholic area. There were Germans in the vicinity who needed someone to minister to them. Mosalkow remembered Erich Schneider, a devout man of God who had been his tent manager when he was preaching for the German Evangelische Tent Mission, and recommended him for the work.

The EES approved support for Schneider to begin an evangelistic work among his own people. He dug a baptistery in his back yard and in just a short time baptized eleven believers. He also started a children's home in faith that somehow the finance needed for this enterprise would be met in the Lord. Alas, eventually, Deelstra persuaded Schneider to relinquish his connection with the EES, and he did. Then, having no source of income, Schneider reversed his decision, but too late. Schneider had no other recourse than to return to Germany.

God, however, was not unmindful of the work begun in Genk and had been preparing another worker to labor in His vineyard there. Dr. Floyd Clark, professor at Johnson Bible College, wrote Earl about a young Frenchman, Don Castelein, who was completing his studies at the college and was interested in working for the Lord in Europe. His story is an interesting one.

Don Castelein had met an American soldier during the war called Don Sharp and they had become friends. Several years passed. Sharp trained for the ministry but had not forgotten his friend, who, by this time, had become a journalist, and was able to get in touch with him again. They corresponded. Sharp told Castelein about his faith and life in Jesus Christ. Castelein listened. It sounded like a good story. Sharp said to Castelein that he had a message for him and suggested that he visit him in France. Johnson Bible College students raised money for Sharp to go there and kept an around the clock prayer vigil while he was in France.

When he arrived, Castelein commented, "You were that interested in me? You must have an important message to spend so much money, and have so many people praying." Step-by-step, Sharp led Castelein through the Bible. As they reasoned together, Castelein became convinced that he, too, wanted to be a Christian and was baptized by Don Sharp who arranged for him to study at Johnson Bible College.

Since Castelein spoke Flemish, it was thought that he might be able to help with the work in Genk, Belgium. Earl and Mosalkow arranged to meet Castelein there. Dr. Deelstra agreed to let Castelein, who had his own financial support, work alongside him with the Flemish congregation in October 1956. A relatively new Christian, he eventually differed with Deelstra on some matters of policy and decided to work independently. He threw all of his energy into his work.

It was a mining area. At first there were only two people interested, but soon a viable group of believers came together under Castelein's leadership. No person lived too far for him to reach and he constantly made hospital calls. People with problems sought him out. He was overworked and had little sleep. The group of believers decided to build their own meeting place. The basement was completed first and they met there for a time. Then tragedy struck. Returning home after a strenuous day, Castelein collapsed on the sidewalk in front of his home and died of a heart attack.

For a while, Herr H. Boonaerts and R. Vandebuerie worked with the group who were now bereft of a leader until help came to carry on. Shortly before our return to the U.S. in 1968, Earl was invited to Genk to ordain the elders of the growing congregation. He was also invited to speak. Choosing as a sermon title "Let the Lord Have His Way with You" (Acts 12), he translated his sermon himself from English into German so that all could understand. It was an anniversary service for this church founded by Don Castelein. Years later, Earl walked into Moody Book Store in Johnson City, TN. A man behind the counter called him by name and told him that twenty-five years ago he had heard him speak in a church in Genk, Belgium!

6.
The Pflegenest (Children's Home)

Having no children of their own, my foster brother, Allen Cull, and his wife, Gladys, were eager to adopt a German child. A few blocks away from our apartment was the Pflegenest, a home where Frau Hartman and her family cared for babies ten days to two-years-old. We often visited the home. One day, an eighteen-month-old pretty little blond girl called Christa was brought in. The Culls were informed that the child might be available for adoption. That was confirmed, and Allen, now an engineer living in Mobile, Alabama, went to Tübingen where he arranged for the adoption of Christa Friedl Kull in 1956. They didn't even have to change the last name, just the spelling—from Kull to Cull.

Army Chapel groups in Ludwigsburg and Böblingen became interested in the Pflegenest after inquiring of us about some project they might undertake to help German people. The Hartman home needed to be renovated, we told them, so that more efficient care could be given to the babies. They brought in equipment and manpower and fixed it up.

After a reporter interviewed Earl about the renovation of the home, an article about an anonymous benefactor (Earl) appeared in the local newspaper. It must be said here that the journalist had written an article about the help of Americans, naming them, in the renovation project for the paper the previous week. The following is a translation of the article which appeared in the *Schwaebisches Tagblatt*:

No Thanks Wanted for a Good Deed Done

Meeting and a conversation with an American who would not let his name be used as one who had done a good deed.

On the last Saturday in the old year (1956), the Turmer (the writer of this article) met an American. The purpose of their meeting was to speak of a certain good deed which should not be named here because it concerns the question namely: that a good deed should not be done because of thanks and honor one might receive in doing it, if it is to be a truly good deed. There could scarcely be a better theme for the first weekend in the new year. One could actually say that it was by accident that it was an American whom the Turmer has to thank for the idea. But it should not go unnoticed that one tends to think of someone from the new world—as the United States was often referred to earlier—a serious, thoughtful and calculating business man, who does nothing which does not bring reward.

In conversation with the Turmer, this American named a long list of names—names of his fellow-countrymen who had helped in any little way with the project about which we spoke. But one felt that he should have been named in the first line. And that he would not allow under any circumstances. It goes without saying that his wish must be respected but the wish left the Turmer reflecting in the following days how much unselfishness there is in a work when one remains so much in the background that afterwards no one knows anything about him or has no idea how much effort he has put forth. One brushes against few who do good deeds without thanks, rewards and that it is known. It is good to examine our motives with the ideal in mind when we do a good deed.

Everyone who thinks these are empty words may be right. The American would include all in his appreciation, even those who did the least. It is earnest with him when he said that in striving to do a good deed it is very important that one have pure satisfaction within and without in the little things as well as the big. The partner in conversation with the Turmer said it in a few simple words that the important thing in doing a good deed is that it will be done, never mind who does it.

In that the American names his fellow-countrymen is a possible contradiction for he named not only them but also the Germans who had any part in the project. Above all, he did not want one party of those who helped to have more honor than another but rather that there was togetherness in the work and a mutual desire to help in mastering and overcoming the need. As soon as it was discovered that the several parties helped, already one knew that the anonymous one was in the background and the "Gemeinshaft" (community) takes on the responsibility and rewards in which the individuals have contributed.

Therein is to be found the true love of one's neighbors when one undertakes to help another to the best of his ability and wishes no thanks, mention, or honor for himself. What happens in a private life is revealed also in his public life and in the higher circles of life. True, there belongs much examination of oneself and striving. Not everyone is able to do this and what they do should not be belittled. Yet the Turmer is not meaning to write in cold, brutal words as unthankful but that only that one should not think of himself first in order to do a good deed. In the willingness to do a good deed without honor or thanks for the sake of doing it, all the secrets are kept buried and in the word "love" the most beautiful and pure meaning is experienced. About this, one could say much, but this is not the right hour. It can be saved for another time.

7.
Activities in the Christliche Gemeinde

Rosemarie Dietrick was an assistant to the head doctor of the Medizienische Klinik in Tübingen. She had come a few years earlier with her family from the East Zone. In Tübingen, she was introduced to the Intervarsity Movement through which she became a dynamic Christian, using even her lunch hours to initiate prayer and Bible study groups on the University campus. She heard about the fellowship of Christians meeting in Gartenstraße and visited the group, bringing other SMD (Intervarsity) students with her. One in particular was Karl Heinz Goll, a former Hitler youth with a lot of questions and doubts about the viability of Christianity. Actually, it was only through counseling which helped him to reverse some of his brain-washed ideas that he eventually was able to claim Christ as Savior.

Rosemarie and Karl eventually married and Earl and Mosalkow were invited to participate in the ceremony at the home of Rosemarie's parents near Pforzheim. This couple has continued as a part of the Christliche Gemeinde ever since and, for the most part, has filled leadership roles, traveling some fifty miles from Pforzheim to Tübingen for services. Karl Heinz became a teacher of history and English in a high school. They had three children.

Before his retirement, Karl suffered health problems. I wrote about an incident that happened to him once for a monthly paper, *First Ladies*, published by the Women's Council of First Christian Church in Johnson City, TN. in October 1988 for a column titled "His Wonders to Perform."

> In my lifetime I have known two persons who have been critically ill from brain hemorrhage—both male, both Christians—and both miraculously survived!
> In the case of one of these, Karl Heinz Goll, an English and history teacher in a German high school in Pforzheim, Germany, the healing is attributed directly to prayer which began during the time it was discovered he was "missing."
> Although he has no memory of his action, Karl Heinz was driving along the autobahn between Stuttgart and Pforzheim and had enough presence of mind, when he wasn't feeling well, to pull off onto a shoulder of the road, get out of the car, and lie down on the grass. Several hours later, he

was found unconscious but alive. He was rushed to the hospital in Stuttgart where the diagnosis was serious brain hemorrhage. For days he hung between life and death, oblivious to all that went on about him.

Meanwhile, members in the Christliche Gemeinde in Tübingen, his home church, prayed and searched the Scriptures for instructions as to how they could help. James 5:14–15 seemed to "speak" to them in that hour. And so Josef Schauer and Giesela Kohlen were chosen to go to the bedside of Karl Heinz with oil for an anointing and for prayer while others kept a prayer vigil at home.

At the hospital, they found Karl Heinz in intensive care, his head swathed in bandages, no part of which was exposed for them to touch. Anyhow, he would be completely unaware of their presence, they reasoned, and so they placed their hands on his hands, prayed, and slipped out of the room.

Back in Tübingen, Dina Luik had a vision. At the very time that Gisela and Josef were praying for Karl Heinz in the hospital, she was "holding his head in her hands" and God was healing it! Several weeks later, Karl Heinz was at home with his family and after some months he was in his classroom again.

Although Karl Heinz remembered nothing else during those early days in the hospital, he could recall that "somebody" came and prayed. Recently, while in Tübingen, I heard him say to Dina, "You held my head in your hands, and I will thank you forever."

God uses many ways His wonders to perform. We can rejoice that we know Him as Lord and Savior, always listening and responding.

One young lady, Fraulein Ingebourg Proehle, more than any other, told the people in the community about becoming a Christian and thus helped greatly in the work of the Christliche Gemeinde.

She said of her baptism, "It was the most important decision I ever made."

Fraulein Ingebourg had fled Hungary with her father who had been a professor of Oriental and Semitic languages at Budapest University. She received the typical European aristocratic education with first-class private teachers who taught her and her siblings in their home. She first came to services in the Gartenstrasse with a young woman who was secretary to the famous psychologist, Dr. Kretchmer, in Tübingen.

Her one-room apartment was cluttered with easels, paints, and canvases, for she was a "Kunst Malerin" (visual artist). One of her favorite pictures depicts her fleeing from Hungary. She called it "From Darkness to Light." It humiliated her to have to take money for her work as an artist. She said it was like selling her soul. Often she exchanged her paintings for a service she needed. She painted a portrait of a dentist's wife in payment for having a badly needed dental job done.

Johannas Stupp, from Latvia, finished his ministerial training at the University of Tübingen. Knowing that it would be difficult for him to serve as a minister in Germany, he also studied for a degree in education. Wilfried Biering baptized him in 1951. Stupp won a scholarship to study the relationship between school and church in Sweden, and received his doctorate at Bonn University where he was interpreter for the Bonn Government for a time. We kept in touch during the succeeding years. He worked with exiled students at Bad Godesburg near Bonn. Interested in propagating the cause of Christ among students there, he arranged for a conference and invited Earl, Dr. Mosalkow and Fritz Schmitt to participate.

Johannes married a physician and they had one son. In 1957 they moved to Erlangen where he took a position as supervisor of the Alexandrium, a student residence at the University of Erlangen and planned the cultural activities. He invited Earl there for a lecture in 1959. On the last Sunday before we returned to the U.S. in 1968, Stupp was ordained by the Christliche Gemeinde in Tübingen. It was his desire to have ecumenical services for the students at the Alexandrium. He remained with that institution until his retirement in the spring of 1988.

Sundays were always busy days, with a full schedule and sometimes surprises. I was up early to bake communion bread, cook dinner for invited guests and sometimes unexpected ones, too, and to plan for Kuchen and coffee in the afternoon at which time musicians in the city had a standing invitation to come and play. In addition to preaching, Earl provided transportation for those living out of town who wished to attend services and often did calling in the late afternoon when families returned home from outings.

In later years I described one "Hausmusik" program on a Sunday afternoon. Although there was an open invitation to families interested in music, sometimes only our family was present for the music. On this occasion, Jane had baked a red velvet cake. Frl. Gertrud Maliga, Jane's speech teacher who was once an actress, and John Estes, a University of Kansas student studying in Tübingen, were our surprise guests.

"Coffee" was always served around the coffee table in the living room. Since Earl Lee and John were eager to play ping pong, Hausmusik began immediately following coffee. Earl Lee played the guitar for everyone to sing Negro spirituals. Fraulein Maliga quoted a poem about Michael Angelo in German. John read a poem by Keats in English, while Loren recited a seasonal poem he had learned at school in German and played a number on the zither. Jane, father Earl, and Dale played a trio for piano, violin, and saw: "Komm, Lieber Zither, Komm." The last contribution was a recorder quartet accompaniment while I sang "I Walk with the King." After driving Frl. Maliga home and eating a light supper, Earl was able to turn his thoughts to other things.

The older children did their school assignments and Loren had a story read to him before going to bed. I co-signed some invitations to high officials of the state and city for a reception sponsored by the German American Club. Frequently, several of our many faceted activities were accomplished on the same day.

There were times, however, when we felt very much alone in our efforts and longed for Christian fellowship with others who shared our vision for the work in Europe. We could understand the value of missionaries going out in teams. One day, Earl looked out the window of his study and saw a man approaching the house. Thinking he was a friend from home, he called me and we were ready to receive him with open arms. It was a disappointment when the "mirage" turned out to be a local insurance agent!

It was no mirage, however, when Dr. John McCaw, Dean of Drake Divinity School in Des Moines, Iowa, and member of the Christian Church (Disciples of Christ) visited Tübingen in 1958. He wanted to meet with some of the professors of the Theological Faculty at Tübingen University and wrote Professor Otto Michel who was serving as dean at the time and so the Faculty of Theology called on Earl for help. They often did this, whether it was to translate an article, interpret for an English speaking person, or to obtain information about a visiting American theologian.

Since McCaw needed an interpreter, Michel asked Earl to meet McCaw at the Bahnhoff (train station) and interpret for him in his interviews with faculty members. One evening during his visit, we invited him and Otto Betz, at that time Dozent (assistant professor) in the Tübingen Faculty of Theology, for dinner. An interesting discussion ensued as to the existence of the devil.

There was great rejoicing when James and Donna Crouch joined the work of the EES 1961–1967. James became the minister of the church and learned the language well. Donna, a professionally trained vocalist, touched the heartstrings of the community when she gave two public concerts at the Amerika

Haus. James and Donna, with their young family, Susan, David and Jeffery, were of great encouragement to the work. In addition to serving as minister of the Gemeinde, James was accepted at the university as a PhD candidate and eventually received his degree there, under the direction of Prof. Dr. Peter Stuhlmacher.

8.
Conferences and Congresses

Early in August, 1959, Earl attended the Annual Conference of the British Churches of Christ in Chester, England. It was the last time he saw Dr. William Robinson, his esteemed professor. He was the Robinsons' overnight guest in Birmingham and rode with them to the conference. "The next decade will be the Decade of Decision," Earl told the British people, intimating that the Disciples of Christ would be undergoing restructure of their total administrative functions as a church denomination. This was put into effect in 1969 at the Convention of Disciples of Christ in Kansas City, Ronald Osborn, president.

Not long after returning from England, Earl was off again, this time as fraternal delegate to the World Convention of Churches of Christ to the German Church Congress known as the Kirchentag which was being held on August 12–16 in Munich. This post-war movement had begun in 1950 to rally the members of the Lutheran, Reformed, and other Protestant churches in Germany for periodic assemblies of fellowship, study, and witness.

At the First Baptist Church in Indianapolis, Indiana, Earl had heard Dr. von Thadden-Trieglaff tell about the Kirchentag and asked him how it had originated. He had stood erect, clicked his heels, bowed his head, and replied: "I am the creator and founder of the Kirchentag."

The Kirchentag had indeed filled a void. A well-educated young German once told Earl: "As a country we have no past to be proud of." That sentiment revealed the state of depression into which the younger generation of Germans had fallen. Into that vacuum of disillusionment and uncertainty stepped the Kirchentag.

July 1958, Earl and Dr. Mosalkow attended the Congress of European Baptists in Berlin where they met several leaders of the Evangelical Christians and Baptists from Russia. For Mosalkow, this association held a special meaning. After forty-seven years, he saw again his close friend from his youth, Jakob Zhidkow, in the church in Moscow. Jakob was now President of the Union of Evangelical Christians and Baptists in the Soviet Union. Mosalkow interpreted for Zhidkow at two church services in the East Sector of Berlin which they visited the last Sunday of July.

In these and other sessions, Zhidkow told about the work in Russia. During the war, the two major evangelical streams in Russia united in one union of Evangelical Christians and Baptists. It left individual churches, however, free to follow the apostolic order. They embraced 550,000 baptized believers in 5,280 churches. Each church had a pastor but relied also on others to preach. The pastors were selected from those presbyters and deacons who had previously qualified themselves in preaching and in the leadership of the church. About 12,000 a year were baptized, all being over eighteen years of age. The state forbade baptism of a believer under eighteen. The churches required an individual to prove his faithfulness a year before baptism. The Lord's Supper was observed at least on the first Sunday of each month, and every Lord's Day in some of the churches. So long as the churches did not form special groups of youth, men, or women, and restricted public services to authorized premises, they were allowed to go about their witness and work.

When Earl asked Brother Karew, the general secretary of the Union, if they had a Bible seminary, he replied: "Yes, as many seminaries as churches. Each church is a training center for its own preachers." He added, however, that they would not be averse to having a separate and distinct Bible seminary if they had the teachers and resources for it. Some of their young men had attended Spurgeon's College in London.

The Union in Russia had never attached itself to any outside association, not even to the Baptist World Alliance, though it had become closely related to the Baptists through their interest in the Russian movement. In Europe, the Baptists, some two-thirds of a million strong, were the closest to the Union of Evangelical Christians and Baptists in Russia, so that it was only natural that they had grown together.

The leaders of the Union were aware of the Christian Churches with which Prochanow conversed in his two visits to the United States, the last being in 1935, shortly before his death. They would welcome more fellowship with these churches. We felt it important for the EES to develop a relationship with the Russian Evangelical Movement while the link with Mosalkow still existed.

9.
Institute for the Study of Christian Origins and the Birth of Loren Theo

1960 was an eventful year. In the first place, our fourth child, Loren Theo, was born April 7 in the Tübingen Frauen Klinik. There were three happy siblings to rejoice at his birth, in addition to his parents and many friends in the church and city, and, I'm sure, a multitude of heavenly angels as well. His Stuckenbruck grandmother wrote: "Thank you for the picture of little Loren. We would like to have his IQ." Jane gave him "motherly" attention. As he grew, she tried to teach him everything she was learning, including piano.

1960 saw not only the birth of our fourth child but also the birth of the Institute for Research in Church Origins. (Dr. Scott Bartchy later changed "Church Origins" to "Christian Origins.") It was at Christmas of that year that we invited Dean E. Walker, Milligan College president in Tennessee, and Burton Thurston, who was teaching at American University in Beirut, Lebanon, to come to Tübingen in order to draw up plans for this Institute. As funds were not forthcoming for a college in conjunction with the local university as first envisioned, it was decided that an institute would best fit our needs. There were already many institutes in the area—specialized entities for research and publication. Some were connected with the University, but there were also some that were not. The EES institute could exist as a private institute for research in Christian Origins and would fit into the academic community.

Earl was very familiar with the Institute Judiacum, headed by Professor Otto Michel. And so we could understand how the EES institute, even a private one, could fit into the local system and would be able to accomplish its purpose. Dr. William L. Thompson, director of the EES, came to Tübingen and signed the agreement.

Earl continued building up the Institute with a specialized library in Christian origins, and its listing was included in the catalogue of the University of Tübingen and also at Emmanuel Christian Seminary in the States. In the meantime, Earl initiated a colloquium which met irregularly at the Institute. After we returned to the Sates, however, it met at the university with Professor Otto Betz as faculty co-sponsor.

Meanwhile, we needed a building for the EES work in Tübingen. In 1961, a Fiat dealer came to us wanting the land which the EES had purchased on which to build a college. Earl told him that we were not so much concerned with making money by the sale of the property as we were with being able to acquire a building for the proposed Institute.

In the autumn of that year, the Fiat dealer approached Earl again, this time with the offer of exchanging the EES land for a house at Wilhelmstrasse 100. The house was only a half mile from the center of the university. William L. Thompson, executive director of the EES, was in Tübingen to witness the exchange on February 16, 1962. God truly provided for our needs. It can be said that our facility in Tübingen was bought by the Disciples of Christ in that the land had been purchased with funds raised by A.E. Cory for the Men and Millions Movement, an organization of the Disciples.

The four-story "villa" was a multi-purpose building. Not only did it house The Institut zur Erforschung des Urchristentums, with its excellent library in primitive Christianity, it was also used for research seminars, worship services, and other related meetings, including colloquiums. The Institute is highly visible on a main street leading into the city and it has been a gathering place for people from many nations. God is watching and listening to what happens there, and so are people throughout the world.

Chapter Eleven
Furlough and Final Years in Tübingen

We had been on the field for nine years without a furlough. Now that Jim and Donna Crouch had joined us, it was arranged for the children and me to be in the States for a year. Earl accompanied us to the US but after a short time he returned to Tübingen. We rented our apartment in Tübingen to Gerhardt and Joan Krodel, a professor's family who were on sabbatical. Earl had sleeping quarters at the Institute building.

Earl, Earl Lee, Ottie Mearl, Loren, Dale, & Jane.

I chose for the children and me to spend our furlough in Lake City, Iowa, near the children's Stuckenbruck grandparents and Aunt

Louroe. The children were able to bask in the love and attention of their grandparents and to attend American schools. They provided music on their recorders for programs where I spoke. Maria Reinhardt, a teenager from Tübingen, joined us and eventually was able to get a job under the supervision of Millie Anderson, a nurse, in Fort Dodge.

W. L. Thompson, director of EES operations Stateside, and his wife, Edythe, loaned us a car which greatly facilitated our transportation needs. All in all, it was a rewarding year, marred only by Earl's absence. At the end of the twelve months, we returned to Tübingen for another five years.

During the coming months and years, in so far as participation in the church and institute allowed, Earl decided to concentrate on a specialized theme of study. He was drawn increasingly to the importance of late Judaism for the background of the Gospel and the Church. He had given this area special emphasis in our acquisitions for the library of the Institute. To make the best use of this library, one would need to know the Semitic languages which Earl did. Eventually, he felt led, as his research project, to probe in-depth the Joel quotation in Acts 2.

In 1968, it was decided that it was necessary for us to return to the States. Five years had passed since our last furlough. A foundation had been laid and the work was ready for new personnel. It was important for us to now consider what was best for our children. They needed to learn to know their own country and culture, especially Jane, since she was hearing-impaired.

Hilde Actstetter and American co-president, Marion Porteous of the German-American Women's Club, sponsored a farewell banquet at a restaurant downtown. Many in the community were invited, including city and university officials. Following several speeches, a book of letters from friends who had studied in Tübingen and also some from local people was given to us—a treasured gift! Mayor Doege presented us with "keys to the city," and an invitation to go and come as we pleased!

The following evening, the president of Baden-Wuertenberg, President Birn and his wife, invited us for an additional dinner and presented us with a beautifully illustrated book about the area. And, of course, our beloved Gemeinde hosted a farewell program. We knew the ties that bound us together would not be broken, for Jesus would hold us together. Mixed feelings surfaced. I had spent nearly half my life overseas. We had learned to know and love the German people. We were bonded with them, and we were aware that to return to our own country now would mean a lot of adjustment, but we had confidence that our loving, caring Heavenly Father, our constant Companion, would continue to be our guide and helper.

The following article appeared in the *Suedwest Presse, Schwaebisches Tagblatt,* June, 1968:

He Had a Magic Word
Stuckenbrucks Return to America

In 1946 when Earl Stuckenbruck was sent to Europe by the American church, Disciples of Christ, he had no idea that he would be in Tübingen for such a long time. As he now returns home after twenty years in Tübingen, the good wishes of all those who sought his advice and help go with him. Earl Stuckenbruck practiced brotherly love, quite without the support of authority, without special position. On his own initiative and with an ever growing love of his fellow-man, he went about his work, strengthened by his religious responsibilities. Many have been recipients of his help: people in all walks of life and all nationalities who came together here in Tübingen. He found a magic word for each individual who came to him under emotional stress and with various other questions and problems.

We also say farewell to his wife, Ottie Mearl, president of the German-American Women's Club for many years. She made it her responsibility to bring American new-comers (students and professors) into contact with German families. These number about 50 families each year.

The Stuckenbruck family will be leaving soon for America where Earl Stuckenbruck will be teaching theology at Milligan College in Johnson City, Tennessee. From our hearts, we wish them "alles Gute" for a new beginning. (No author was named and this was translated from the German language.)

Chapter Twelve
Adjusting to Life in America

July 2, 1968, we boarded the *Bremen* at Bremerhaven, Germany, for our journey home. The trip was pleasant. The children were kept busy as they participated in activities on the ship. Earl Lee and Jane entered a talent show and won first place in a ballroom dancing contest.

On the day we landed in New York, the purser on the ship handed us a letter from Leonard Wymore, Director of the North American Christian Convention convening in Cincinnati. He and his wife, Thelma, offered to make their home available so that we could attend the convention. We had not made specific plans as to where we would go after arriving in the States, and so that was a very much appreciated solution.

Upon disembarking the *Bremen*, we were surprised and pleased to meet Scott Bartchy and his wife, Diane. Scott was finishing up his doctorate at Harvard and hoped eventually to work under the auspices of the EES in Tübingen. Meeting them and learning more about their desire to serve in Tübingen was confirmation that the work would continue in the hands of capable people.

We inquired of a cab driver, who seemed to have an honest face, if he would drive us to an inexpensive hotel. Near the hotel was a drug store where we were able to introduce the children to the much talked about milkshakes. The menu chart was confusing. Does one eat "hot dogs" and are "hamburgers" people who live in Hamburg? There was no 13th floor at the hotel! So much confusion! At bedtime, Jane burst into tears and wanted to know if we could go back to Germany. Earl Lee, though already homesick himself, sat on her bed and tried to comfort her. "Everything will be all right," he told her. And it was.

We took a train to Cincinnati where we were met by the Wymores who drove us to their home. Their daughter, Kathy, had made a German chocolate cake! Their kind hospitality coupled with seeing friends at the convention warmed our hearts and helped to make the transition easier.

At the convention, we met Dr. Richard Phillips, a faculty member at Milligan College, and his wife, Becky, who invited us to stay in their home in Johnson City, Tennessee, until we could find a house in the area which we could call home. We hoped to settle in Tennessee as Earl planned to join the faculty at Milligan College, Earl's preference over Puget Sound Christian College, Washington State, and Wheaton College in Illinois, all three colleges having offered him an opening to teach.

Emmanuel School of Religion, a seminary in East Tennessee, was in its beginning stage and the board was selecting the faculty. Dean E. Walker, president of Milligan College and Emmanuel School of Religion, had written to Earl: "As you know, the ESR Board voted to extend a call to you for appointment to the Emmanuel faculty. At that time, we were thinking of an interim period of x years. This invitation, of course, still holds. It would be helpful, however, to know whether you would entertain an invitation to a permanent appointment to the Emmanuel faculty." Earl, with a heart for young people, decided that he would rather teach at Milligan College where younger students were beginning their studies in preparation to becoming Christian leaders.

With Earl's position at Milligan College secure, we turned our attention to our children and to my finding a job to supplement our income. We were well aware that it would take time for the children to adjust, not only to the culture, but also to the school system. Such is the experience of the children of missionaries and foreign diplomats when they return home.

Earl Lee, our oldest son, passed the GED but did not feel that his English was good enough to enter college. He chose to work as an orderly at the Memorial Hospital in Johnson City. His number was called up for him to join the army. He didn't mind serving our country but he did not want to be in a position to kill anyone. With the help of a letter written by Congressman James H. Quillen in his defense, Earl Lee entered the army as a conscientious objector and trained as a medic, graduating as the "Outstanding Trainee" in his class.

It was decided that Jane, who had been home-schooled and enrolled in a semi-private, bi-lingual Waldorf School in Tübingen, should take two years to complete high school in the States. Although deaf, she was mainstreamed at Science Hill High School in Johnson City. It wasn't long until she was co-accompanist on the piano for the choir and artist for the school newspaper. Rod Sturtz, the music teacher, discovered that she had perfect pitch! In Germany, Jane had had a fine piano teacher, Rolf Sturm, who had prepared her to perform a Mozart concerto with the school orchestra as a farewell gift to the community.

In the Waldorf School, teachers had simply written a description of each pupil's work. No alphabetical letter grades had been given, and so the guidance counselor, Frank Tannewitz, at Science Hill asked that I assist in translating Jane's and Dale's grades into alphabetical letters. Jane finally graduated in the top ten percent of her class.

Dale enrolled in the tenth grade at Science Hill High School. Like Jane, he had been a student in the Waldorf School in Tübingen, which, although academic, encouraged arts and crafts. The boys learned to knit and do all the things that girls usually do, and the girls learned to do woodwork and all the things boys usually do. The school prided itself on educating the whole person.

Dale had learned to play the violin and baroque recorder and so became a member of the Science Hill Orchestra. He received an invitation to attend Blue Hill Summer Music Camp in Maine.

Hearing about the invitation and knowing that Dale would have to raise funds to participate, Dr. Ralph Sims, minister of the Downtown Christian Church in Johnson City, encouraged him to give a concert at the church with Jane accompanying, to raise tuition for the camp. The next year, the Wednesday Morning Music Club provided Dale with a scholarship to attend a summer music camp at the University of the South, where he won a competition in which he performed the Bruch Violin Concerto, No 1, with the camp orchestra. Julie Read, local cellist, took Dale with her to play in the Kingsport Symphony. He was also a member of the original Johnson City Symphony.

Loren was eight years old when we returned to the States. Our home was located in Washington County, and so he attended Cherokee Elementary School. He was the only one of our children who did not have to pay tuition to attend school, for city schools charged a fee to students living outside the city limits. The children in Loren's first grade class in the Waldorf School in Tübingen had had to memorize the first five verses of Genesis in five different languages: English, German, French, Greek and Hebrew. Loren had done this without difficulty as he seemed to have a knack for learning languages. This meant that the transition into an English speaking school was not difficult for him. The fact that he was invited to go from class to class and tell the children about Germany proved an additional confidence builder.

I applied to the city school system for a job. In an interview with Howard McCorkle, superintendent of schools, I was told that the English department at Science Hill High School had received a grant for an assistant, and that I was the first one to be hired for that position. It was an opportunity to learn about the inner workings of an American high school and to understand better how to help Jane and Dale adjust.

As we settled into life in North Eastern Tennessee, we realized that we needed to find a church home. It was our intention to locate a small church in the area and help build it up. However, on our first Sunday in the area, we visited First Christian Church (later Downtown Christian Church) in Johnson City. The children were immediately included in the activities of the young people, and Earl and I also accepted responsibilities. I joined the choir and Earl was elected as an elder. We have loved being a part of the family of God in this congregation. Except for an interim ministry with our beloved Grandview Christian Church, we have been with the Downtown Christian Church (First Christian) for forty-eight years, and counting.

With a longing to learn to know our sisters in Christ in other area Christian Churches, Donna Sims, Nancy Campbell, Lorraine Brown and I started the Appalachian Christian Women's Retreat and an annual citywide Agape Feast for women. For a dozen years, we enjoyed a broader working relationship and warm fellowship with our sisters in Christ in other churches as well as our own.

Chapter Thirteen
Tübingen not Forgotten

Meanwhile, Tübingen remained in our hearts. We were, of course, prayerfully concerned for the work we had left behind there. Dr. William (Bill) Thompson was Executive Director of the European Evangelistic Society. He was involved in additional ministry as well, serving as senior minister of Lock Haven Church of Christ in Pennsylvania and later Central Christian Church in Pittsburgh, Pennsylvania. "From 1961–1968, he was our Special Representative. From 1968–1976 he was our part-time Representative and Executive Director. From 1977–1981, he was our full-time Executive Director. He held dear the work of the European Evangelistic Society and committed himself unremittingly to its promotion," wrote Dr. Robert Shaw, EES president. "His vision was for the whole Church. His zeal like that of the early reformers was for a Church united," commented William L. Thompson III, minister and Bill's oldest son.

Bill, as he was known by all of us, was interested in the writings of Prof. Dr. Ernst Kaesemann, Prof. Dr. Peter Beyerhaus, and Prof. Dr. Hans Kueng—all professors at Eberhard-Karls Universität in Tübingen. During his visits to Tübingen, Bill became personally acquainted with Prof. Kueng. When he lay dying in a Chicago hospital, Prof. Kueng happened to be visiting in the area. Hearing about Bill's illness, he made his way to the hospital to visit his friend.

When we left Germany, Burton Thurston took leave of his work as head of Religious Studies at the American University in Beirut, Lebanon, so that he could become interim Director of the

Institute in Tübingen and in charge of the EES work abroad. Earl had been serving as Director of the Institute and minister of the church. A German couple, Wolfgang and Rosemarie Stoll, took over the ministry of the Gemeinde (church). Wolfgang had finished his theological exams at Hamburg University. Rosemarie was trained as a social worker.

In 1969, Scott and Diane Bartchy arrived in Tübingen with their children, Beth and Chris, to assume leadership of the EES work. In addition to Scott's being Director of the Institute and having a "Lehrauftrag" (contract) to teach at the University, he and Diane brought into existence the Gerdtell Haus for international students. "Dr. Ludwig von Gerdtell gave American Christians a strong personal invitation to join him in his concern for the future of the Christian faith and life in his homeland," wrote Scott Bartchy. "He sought to share with them his vision: that the Church of Germany's future would be the Church of the New Testament." An average of nine students lived in this large house with Scott and Diane, as a sort of extended family, and each paid his or her share of the rent. It was a valuable ministry through which the Bartchy family was able to broaden their influence for our Lord Jesus Christ.

Dr. Fred Norris, a Yale PhD, and his wife, Carol, and their two children, Mark and Lisa, arrived in Tübingen in 1972 and served until 1977. Part of the time, Fred was Director of the Institute. In addition, he taught courses at the University of Tübingen while Carol taught school. They also worked with the Christliche Gemeinde.

Bruce Shields, a Milligan College and Princeton Theological Seminary graduate, his wife Rosemarie, and their three children, Karen, James and Robert, arrived in Tübingen in 1972 and served at their own expense. Wolfgang and Rosemarie Stoll had moved on and so Bruce became minister of the Christliche Gemeinde and worked with Prof. Dr. Peter Stuhlmacher as his "doctor father."

Rosemarie taught school and tutored students and professionals in English, in addition to helping in the Gemeinde.

Scott and Diane, Fred and Carol, and Bruce and Rosemarie were all Milligan College graduates. Part of the time they were all serving together in Tübingen. Bruce has said that it took three families to do the many facets of the work that the Stuckenbrucks had been doing, and he was right. At the same time, however, the three families added some new dimensions: they taught at the university; they moved the colloquia to the university campus with a co-sponsor, Prof. Otto Betz, of the University faculty, and they increased awareness of the EES's existence in the community.

Meanwhile, back in the States, James L. Evans had left his position as professor of New Testament Language and Literature at Atlanta Christian College to succeed William (Bill) L. Thompson as Executive Director of the European Evangelistic Society in 1982. Like Bill, Jim kept abreast of what was happening in Tübingen and presented the information to churches in the U.S. for the purpose of prayer concern and raising funds for the work. It was an arduous task and he was dedicated to the cause. It has been amazing how those who are convinced that God has a purpose in promoting Christian unity, according to the Scriptures, have been able to achieve so much considering the slim budget at their disposal. No other instance of a foreign, church-based, research-oriented institute with close ties to a university and with its own faculty of theology exists in Germany. Here also is a rare outworking of biblical witness by Christian Churches among wider academic circles in Christendom.

Jim and his wife, Ellen, worked closely with Dr. Robert Shaw, EES president, following the resignation of President Dr. Dean E. Walker in 1974, and Dr. Bruce Shields, who succeeded Robert Shaw as EES president. It is not easy to raise funds for a mission whose focus is on research and renewal. But, as the song goes, "When it looked like the sun wouldn't shine any more, God put a rainbow in the sky." Robert Shaw knew a lot of people and he had a way of convincing them that what was being done in Tübingen was God's work! They wanted *it* to continue, and they gave—not millions, but enough to help the work survive. Several times during his presidency, Robert literally saved the work by finding people who gave. He and Virgie Lee, his wife, gave liberally also. In addition, Robert promoted order in board meetings. This was made easier by the fact that Virgie Lee was a parliamentarian and knew the value of order in getting work done efficiently.

Over the years, lack of funds for the work of the EES has always plagued the efforts of those involved and, eventually, Scott and Diane returned to the U.S. and Scott accepted a position as professor of church history at UCLA. Likewise, Fred and Carol accepted a position at Emmanuel School of Religion. Bruce received his doctorate and accepted a position at Lincoln Christian Seminary and later at Emmanuel School of Religion.

Chapter Fourteen
Changes in the Family

Jane's main interest was music. She was proficient in piano, flute, and recorder and auditioned to study piano at the North Carolina School for the Performing Arts in Winston Salem, North Carolina. Facing leaving home for the first time, she wanted to assure her father and me that she could cope with everyday challenges in the "hearing world." And so she painted a mural of Jesus stilling the storm on the Sea of Galilee on a basement wall in our family home. "Don't worry about me," she said upon departing for college. "I know it will not be easy, but Jesus will always be there stilling the storms." There have been many times when we needed to remember that picture and allow it to confirm her words.

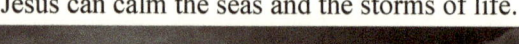
Jesus can calm the seas and the storms of life.

Jane and her painting.

Since the school Jane was applying to also accepted high school students, Dale auditioned as well and completed his senior year in high school as well his B.A. degree at NCSA. Both received tuition scholarships, plus other stipends.

It was a difficult decision to leave both Jane and Dale at NCSA when they registered at the conservatory, knowing that they would be entering a completely secular environment; but, realizing the quality of teaching and exposure to "the greats" in the classical music world, we consented. Because of Earl's teaching schedule, I drove Jane and Dale to enroll when school started. Walking down one of the dorm halls, I saw a rubber chicken hanging over a sink in a semi-lighted room and met a male student with half of his head shaven. Was this the environment we wanted for our children? Dare I leave them there?

I took the Blue Ridge Parkway home, the closest physical route to heaven, and wept most of the way. I chided myself, wondering if we had made the right decision. Soon, however, Dale and Jane discovered Christian friends and others who were striving to succeed in their particular areas of the arts. In particular, they met Trudy Nifong and her family who took them under her wings. Dale and Jane met once a week to call home. Both would speak on the phone. Dale would tell Jane what we said.

Meanwhile, Earl Lee was honorably discharged from the army, due to health issues, and became a much sought-after piano tuner technician. He had had eight years of piano lessons and began tuning, following a correspondence course with the Aubrey Willis School of Piano Tuning, Regulating, and Repairing, in Orlando, Florida, in 1976. He was apprenticed to Clayton Harmon, his career "father," in Asheville, North Carolina. Later, having spent two sessions of training at the Steinway Factory in New York, he became an All Steinway School Technical Partner tuner and continued tuning for East Tennessee State University when the school became an all Steinway Music Department. In addition, he demonstrated through examination that he fulfilled the requirements of technical competence to become a registered piano technician and belonged to the Piano Technicians Guild. "Registered Piano Technicians" it was stated, "are professionals who have committed themselves to the continual pursuit of excellence, both in technical service and ethical conduct."

Dale and Jane had excellent tutelage at the conservatory: Jane under Rebecca Penney for piano, and Dale with Erick Friedmann for violin. They received their degrees with honors and moved on. Jane concertized and taught music at Roanoke Bible College and then became an interim teacher of piano at Milligan College after she completed a master's degree at Samford University in Birmingham, Alabama. Her teacher there, Betty Sue Shepherd, built on the foundation laid by Rebecca Penney. Sometimes, when Mrs. Shepherd had to be away, she would ask Jane to teach her freshman students. Jane also won a competition to perform Beethoven's Concerto, No 4 in G Major with members of the Birmingham Symphony.

Dale finally followed his teacher, Erick Friedmann, to the Manhattan School of Music in New York City where he completed a master's degree and then pursued a Doctor of Musical Arts degree. As concert master and sometimes contractor for the pit musicians for Broadway shows, in addition to performing as soloist with chamber groups and with orchestras, he had little time to work on a doctoral dissertation. Not only did he have a busy schedule performing and teaching, he also wrote articles for the music magazine, *Notes*. However, in the end, Earl helped with typing Dale's dissertation and Heawon, Dale's wife, with copying, and so together, they were able to turn it in just *one minute* before the deadline—a real achievement! Heawon, her daughter, Carin, Earl, and I were in the audience to see Dale hooded for his doctorate.

Following a brief time at Oral Roberts University, Loren enrolled at Milligan College. While there, he commuted to the North Carolina School for the Performing Arts for piano lessons. Upon graduating, Loren enrolled at Butler University where he studied biblical languages and also piano at Arthur Jordan Conservatory. At the same time, he was interim choir director at East 91st Street Christian Church before going on to Princeton Theological Seminary for a Master's degree and eventually a doctorate.

Chapter Fifteen
The Work in Tübingen Continues

In 1981, as Hylda Smith and I listened to EES board members trying to think of ways to raise money for the Tübingen work, we felt led of the Lord to help. Hylda, a minister's wife, with plenty of leadership roles and projects to support, added the EES to her special concerns. Her husband, Frank, had been a long-time member of the EES executive committee. Hylda remembered the example of Phoebe (Romans 16:1) and suggested that available women function as *The Order of the Phoebe*, an auxiliary of the EES. We baked bread, sewed aprons and bed caddies, catered meetings, cleaned homes, and did a number of other things to raise money. Finally, we ran out of steam and counted our earnings for the cause—$17,000 in four years!

Dr. James Thompson, Abilene Christian Seminary, became the Director of the Institute for Research in Christian Origins for a time, followed by Dr. Thomas Best, professor on leave from Butler University. While there, Dr. Best wrote: "It is impossible to separate the life of the Institute from its relationship with the Christian Church in Tübingen. They have grown by the Spirit, and we do not want to quench the Spirit." Dr. Paul Hanson, professor at Harvard Divinity School, also helped with the Institute when he was in Tübingen.

Drs. Burton and Bonnie Thurston served as Directors. Elaine had passed away and Bonnie, a scholar and former student of Burton, became his bride. They served in Tübingen 1983–1985. While Burton's specialty was theology, Bonnie's was spirituality.

She collected a bibliography of scholars, who had been connected with the Institute, and their writings. In addition, she wrote a brief history in which she redefined the EES:

> The Institut zur Erforschung des Urchristentums is basically a research facility providing a library of over 2,000 volumes and forty regular periodicals for the university community and visiting scholars. The EES believes that the origins of the faith are germane not only to Christian theologians, but to Jewish scholars, ancient historians, and linguists. All who follow Christ can benefit from knowledge of the forces that influenced the formation of His Church. To this end, research has been carried out on the major urban centers of early Christianity—Corinth, Antioch, and Ephesus. Topics of sustained investigation have included the Lord's Supper, Baptism, the Holy Spirit, Freedom and Slavery in the Ancient World, the Place of Women in the Church, and the relationship between church life in the 1st and 20th centuries. Dr. Burton Thurston completed a commentary on the history of early Christianity in Cyprus. The list of scholars who have had contact with the Institute would be long and distinguished.

Scott J. Haffeman was an assistant for Scholarly Affairs. Dr. William Howden served as Director with Dr. David A Fiensy as Scholar in Residence. Dr. Ron Heine served the longest as Director of the Institute, followed by Dr. Scott Caulley. As I write, Dr. Beth Langstaff is staff Director. Upon the retirement of James Evans in 2003, Wye Huxford came on board as Executive Director, part of the time as a volunteer! Each has made a significant contribution to the work in Tübingen.

Dr. Bruce Shields became President of the European Evangelistic Society at a ceremony at the World Convention in Calgary, Canada. Three significant things have happened during the time that he has served: He has negotiated, together with Dr. Scott Caulley, a formal relationship of the Institute with the University of Tübingen, helped Dr. Ron Heine and Dr. Scott Caulley with the first Symposium sponsored jointly by the EES and Eberhard-Karls Universität in 2009, and skillfully managed, together with Dr. Tony Twist, a merger of EES with TCM also in 2009.

The Christliche Gemeinde, closely connected to the Institute, also continued to function in the community. Werner M. Hausen, Dennis R. Lindsay, Gennadij Dueck (ordained by the Christliche Gemeinde) and Jim Kautt succeeded Bruce Shields as ministers. Jim and Naomi Kautt have served the longest. Jim has completed his residence work at the University of Tübingen for a doctorate. Naomi, his wife, has completed a second Bachelor's degree in musicology and is a professional singer. The name of the church has been changed to the "International Christian Church—Christliche Gemeinde" and meets at Mohlstrasse 26, 72074 Tübingen, Germany. The church's primary ministry is to international graduate students, but also serves a nucleus of local people who are members. Jim and Naomi can be commended for the far reaching influence of their ministry for Christ.

Wye Huxford is responsible for bringing a Globalscope Team, an additional ministry, under the auspices of the Christian Missionary Fellowship, to Tübingen. Beth Silliman is the popular leader of the group. They met with students (mostly undergraduates) in the Institute building, until 2014, when the University was in session for social events and serious discussions. They are using this unique method of influencing students to come to know and accept Jesus Christ as Savior.

My heart desires that I keep writing about what is happening in Tübingen, but those stories really belong to the personnel who have served since we left. The following is a note from Prof. Dr. Otto Betz, long time German friend, who was featured in the *European Evangelist* in the year 2000:

Isolde and I were touched by your article honoring us in the *European Evangelist,* Spring 2000, telling about some of our experiences together with you over the past nearly fifty years.... Especially do we remember the wonderful people, the president of the European Evangelistic Society and others, we learned to know when they visited you while we were living in the same apartment building in the Schlossbergstrasse in Tübingen....

Working with Professor Heine was a wonderful experience. He organized and led the discussions for the Coloquia at the University.

We are glad that through Loren we can remain in personal contact with you since our ages prevent our visiting back and forth. He will be in Tübingen the beginning of May for a conference of the Pseudepigrapha and will be giving a lecture. Loren is appreciated and loved by his doctoral students in England, America, and Germany.

We are thankful for the Institute and the Gemeinde, sponsored by the European Evangelistic Society, in Tübingen, Wilhelmstr. 100, where there are so many memories of you, especially the library and the large meeting room.

Dr. Heine and Dr. Shields should write more about the Institute and Gemeinde in Tübingen. The American churches of your persuasion are informed, but others there and here in Tübingen do not know enough about them.

Chapter Sixteen
Family Matters

1.
An Eventful Year

1976 was an eventful year for our family. While we were still in Tübingen, Earl did research on *The Joel Quotation in Acts 2:17–21*. He was looking into the background of this quotation in late Judaism and its connection with the Sermon on Pentecost in light of Jewish homilies. He had a sabbatical from Milligan College in 1976 and used the time to continue his research at Hebrew College in Cincinnati, Duke University in North Carolina, and the University of Tübingen in Germany.

Upon returning home, word came that his father, who was in Pomeroy nursing home, near Lake City, Iowa, had become seriously ill and died. His mother had passed away in January of the same year. Earl and his brother, Harry, met in Lake City and prepared a lovely memorial service for their father and then they took him to Tipton, Iowa, for burial. In the meantime, *The Joel Quotation in Acts 2:17–21,* was finished and boxed up, ready for publication. There it has remained to this day.

December 24, 1979, Earl was cleaning the gutters on the back side of our house when his ladder gave way and he fell backwards onto a cement patio. He was taken to the Emergency Room where x-rays revealed that his injuries, though serious, were not life-threatening. He was heavily sedated and admitted to the hospital. Anxious days followed. This was the beginning of many health issues.

It was Christmas Eve and we were invited to celebrate the birthday of Jesus with Herald and Mary Jane Cabus and family. Since Earl was being cared for in the hospital, I decided that the children and I would join the party. Mark and Rand, their children, were always home for the occasion. Mary Jane put together a program which included everyone present with choice readings, beautiful music, and earnest prayers. Of course, there was also a lighted birthday cake, remembering Jesus' birth, and delicious food. For more than thirty years, we celebrated Christmas Eve with this family and with others they invited, until Mary Jane's health eventually failed. It became a memorable part of our Christmas for many years.

It was inevitable that, eventually, our family would expand. Earl Lee, Dale, and Loren added "daughters" to our family, while Jane added a "son." Earl Lee and Connie, a secretary at Mission Hospital, were married at First Christian Church in Asheville, North Carolina, by Rev. Daniel; Dale and Heawon, a Korean child prodigy pianist and graduate of a famous girls' art high school, EWHA, in Korea, with a B.A. degree from the North Carolina School for the Performing Arts and an MA from Manhattan School of Music, were married at Park Ave Christian Church in N.Y. City by Earl; Loren and Lois, who gave up a profession as a ballerina for a double major in business and English Literature and minor in French at Milligan College, were also married by Earl at Hopwood Christian Church on the Milligan College campus. Jane and Robert Perry, whom she met at Samford University, were married at First Christian Church in Johnson City by Jane's father.

Loren, a pianist as well as a scholar, performed the dedication concert for a new $49,000 Bechstein piano February 4, 1985, in Princeton Theological Seminary's Miller Chapel. Not wanting to distract Loren and Lois as they prepared for the big event, we slipped into the chapel unobserved. Our presence was therefore a surprise to Lois, when looking around, she spotted us in the crowded audience. It was a good thing I was able to sit between her and Earl as Loren performed Beethoven, Chopin, and Liszt, for I needed someone to hold on to when the notes tumbled forth sometimes at almost unbelievable speed. The music was so heavenly that without them as my anchor, I felt as though I would surely float away. During the intermission, Loren, behind the stage, thought he heard his father laugh. It couldn't be....it was! Heawon and daughter, Carin, were also present. Dale performed a concert that evening nearby, but was able to join us for the reception at PTS.

September 1, 1984, Dale came to Johnson City to attend his brother's wedding. He brought with him his three-year-old daughter, Carin. Heawon stayed at home in N.Y. to help her sister whose husband was dying of cancer. She met the plane when Dale and Carin returned home. Because Carin was not feeling well, they took her to the ER. Around 11 p.m., they phoned to tell us that Carin had been diagnosed with leukemia!

For the next two years, she was in and out of the hospital. Her parents never left her alone at the hospital. Busy with concerts and teaching, they arranged their schedules so that one of them was with her, even during the nights. The outpouring of love and support by friends and acquaintances was remarkable. Friends even hired taxis to come long distances to give blood as needed. One might think that New York's teeming millions are cold and passive. Not so. Even the doctors became close friends because the young patient drew their loving attention by the things she said and did. She was "in charge" of what happened in her room.

When Dale learned that the end was near, he cancelled his engagements for three weeks to be with Heawon and Carin. The family and some friends gathered round during the last four days of her life. The last thirty-two hours were spent at home on Long Island. From time to time, Carin would call for a family member to come to her bedside and she allowed us to perform some loving act—rub where it hurt, paint her fingernails, read a story. Five-year-old Angela, cousin and friend, and her mother, Jane, were great entertainers.

Two memorial services were held—one at a crowded room at the Wagner Funeral Home in Hicksville with a Korean pastor officiating and a large choir providing the music. A second service took place at the Hicksville Church of Christ with Grandfather Stuckenbruck, her Uncle Loren, and Dr. R. Sturm from Park Ave Christian Church, sharing stories about her life and *hope* in Jesus. Angela and a Korean friend sang, "Little children, little children, who love their Redeemer"—Angela in English and the friend in Korean. It was a precious time of remembering for all the people who filled the sanctuary. Carin was a bit of "heaven come down" and our hearts will ever be filled with joy as we thank God upon every remembrance of her.

Dale and his father found a new cemetery on Long Island, carpeted with green grass, a deep forest in the background, and a new Episcopal church at the entrance. It is the playground for rabbits and birds, a lovely place to rest. At the grave site, it was not like saying "good-bye" to Carin, rather "Aufwiedersehen," until we meet again.

Three times Dale and Heawon have given concerts in Johnson City, in memory of Carin, to benefit the local Hospital Guest House.

As our children were establishing their own homes, we were experiencing empty nest syndrome. However, that didn't last long. Louroe Stuckenbruck, sister of Earl's father, lived in her own home with a friend, Lenore Rutan, in Lake City, Iowa. She had helped to care for Earl's parents until they passed away. She had always been more like an older sister to Earl and his brother, Harry, than an aunt and so she eagerly accepted our invitation to spend winters with us. The routine was that I would fly to Lake City in September and drive her in her car back to Johnson City. As soon as Science

Hill High School, where I worked, was out in the spring, I would drive her back to Lake City and fly home.

She was a favorite person in our family and helped with college expenses for Jane and Dale. She was especially fond of Loren and enjoyed doing special things for him, such as fixing his favorite food. While she was with us in 1983, she passed away. We flew her body to Tipton, Iowa, where she was buried in the Stuckenbruck family section of the cemetery, alongside Earl's parents.

After Loren completed his Master's Degree at Princeton Theological Seminary, he spent two years in Tübingen as a Fulbright Scholar. He and Lois graciously invited Earl and me for a visit. Dale and Heawon made it possible for us financially to accept their invitation. Lois and Loren arranged for us to sublet an apartment at Moerikestr. 11 from December, 1987, to the end of February, 1988.

The first thing we did on arrival was to pick up a Volkswagen Jetta at Wolfsburg which we had ordered before we left the States, saving $1000.00 and shipping expenses to the U.S., thus facilitating our transportation while in Germany.

It was a memorable three months as we entertained local friends, visited with them in their homes, and received family members who flew in from the States for Christmas. We were also able to say good-bye to our dear Tante Else Mosalkow before she went to heaven. She and her husband, Theo, were our beloved co-workers while we were serving in Tübingen. But the really big event was the birth of our granddaughter, Daniella Marie, the first child of Loren and Lois, who was born in the same Klinik as Loren. Jim and Ellen Evans were present our last Sunday in Tübingen when Earl preached at the Christliche Gemeinde to a full house and there was a dedication service for Daniella, with dedicatory prayers by both parents.

2.
Earl Retires

Finally, in 1983, Earl retired. Milligan College honored him with the *Fide et Amore*, the college's Distinguished Service Citation, the contents of which were crafted by Dr. William C. Gwaltney, and I quote:

> Today we honor a gentleman who has served Christ on two continents as scholar, churchman, and minister. The recipient of degrees from the University of Kansas and Butler University School of Religion, Earl Stuckenbruck has pursued his personal quest for knowledge in several of Europe's finest universities, most notably the University of Birmingham, Basel University, and the University of Tübingen. His lifelong research into Christian origins has led to several publications, but more significantly it has contributed to the creation at Tübingen, Germany, of the Institute for Research in Christian Origins. The impact of this institute on theological thought is incalculable.
>
> As a servant of Christ, Professor Stuckenbruck has labored for years in numerous capacities: in the located pastorate, on the mission field (for twenty-one years), in the college and seminar classroom, as elder and teacher in local congregations, and as father, husband, and friend.
>
> But we especially honor him today for his service to Milligan College. While serving on our Bible faculty since 1968, he has set for us all the highest standards in class preparation, love for students, respect for colleagues, and service to all. His enthusiasm is contagious; his nobility, a challenge; his dedication to the good and to God, an inspiration. To work with Earl Stuckenbruck is a joy because he can be counted on to provide an insightful word offered sincerely and humbly.

Milligan is a more stimulating place in which to live, study, and learn because of Earl Stuckenbruck's life among us. He has shown us the higher dimensions of faith and love. For this gift we honor Earl Stuckenbruck this fifteenth day of May, 1983 with the Fide et Amore Award. Signed: W.C. Gwaltney Jr., presented by; Kenneth W. Oosting, for the faculty; Marshall Liggett, president; Charles E. Allen, chairman of the trustees.

When Earl retired, it was decided that I, too, would cease working outside the home. We continued our church activities and also other interests as health allowed. Earl's hobbies were playing the musical saw and musical goblets (glass harp). He tried out many saws in a hardware store and selected one for flexibility and tone quality for his entertainment programs. To select the goblets, he took a little vinegar in a bottle and headed for the glassware department in stores where he got permission to try out goblets. While chatting with customers who were drawn to the sounds, he found enough goblets for three octaves. He was invited to perform on these for civic as well as church meetings. Frank Jarrett, member of First Christian, Johnson City, designed and made three special wooden collapsible tables for the goblets—a useful, remarkable gift—which we could take in the car with us for programs.

Only once did the goblets fail to respond. Earl was invited to play at the Reece Museum, East Tennessee State University, for a Continuing Education group. He had been designated to have the entire program. He set up and prepared the goblets with the proper amount of water and had containers of ascetic acid and vinegar for dipping his fingers to make music on the rims of the goblets.

He introduced the program. We sat in anticipation of hearing beautiful music, but, alas, the glasses would not respond! He tried everything he knew to do, but no music came, only an occasional squeak. A dilemma! A chemist in the audience tried to reason, together with Earl, as to why there was no response. The mystery was never solved. Thankfully, that was the only time it ever happened. Tim Cable, WJHL TV, came to our home for an interview with Earl playing his goblets and used the interview for his "Cable Country" programs a couple of times.

Earl taught Dale to play the musical saw, and now he plays it professionally. He inherited the musical goblets and tables and he, Heawon, and daughter, Erin, continue to use them for classical music programs. Steve Margoshes, composer of the Broadway musical, *Fame*, composed enough music for the musical saw and piano to record a CD, titled "Sawing to New Heights with Steve and Dale." Once when we were visiting Dale, Heawon, and family in N.Y., Dale was scheduled to perform on his saw at a library on Long Island. He invited his father to be a part of the program as a guest. Dale, also a violinist, had been performing in the morning and rushed home to take Earl with him to the library for the program in the afternoon. Alas, he could not find his second saw for Earl to play! What to do? They went to Sears, not far away, and found a saw they could use. Two panting performers arrived just in time to perform as scheduled in front of an appreciative audience!

While Earl was enjoying his hobbies, I was sewing curtains for the dorms at Milligan College, was co-editor with Dorothy Roller and writer for *First Ladies,* a publication of the ladies of First Christian Church, Johnson City. In addition, I sang in the chancel choir, was a speaker at special meetings, and continued to enjoy being a homemaker.

3.
Welcome Home Angela from Uruguay

In the midst of other activities, we drove to Atlanta to welcome Angela, daughter of Jane and Bob, home from Uruguay. February 21, 1996, Bob accompanied his and Jane's daughter, Angela, 14, to Uruguay, South America. There, she was in the care of minister/missionary Ken Schisler and wife, Annie, daughter of Pastor and Mrs. Ed Miller in Atlanta. Bob and Jane visited Angela in Uruguay in June of the same year for one month. In December, we met Bob and Jane in Atlanta to welcome her home. It was a happy day for all of us!

4.
Loren Receives his PhD

It was very special that Earl and I could sit in with Lois for Loren's defense of his dissertation, September 20, 1993. Earl had helped Loren when he was finalizing his doctoral dissertation so that it could be handed in on time. The defense was held in the Conference Room of Templeton Hall. Six professors of Princeton Seminary questioned Loren. They met first on their own to determine procedure. Then Loren, Lois, his wife, Earl and I, together with three PhD candidates, were invited in. With fear and trembling, Loren took his place at the conference table with the professors. The rest of us sat in chairs against the wall. Professor Patrick Miller, moderator for the occasion, broke the first moments of tenseness with prayer.

Loren had chosen as the title of his dissertation: "Do Not Worship Me: Worship God: The Problem of Angel Veneration of Early Judaism and Aspects of Angelmorphic Christology in the Apolalypse of John." Dr. James Charlesworth, Loren's advisor for his dissertation, and Dr. Ulrich Mauser spoke appreciatively of Loren's research and "Zusammen-stellung" (the way he put his findings together) of the material. One said it was the best dissertation he had ever read and the other spoke about how much he learned from reading it. Then the questions began as follows:

"What led you to want to explore the subject of your dissertation? What contribution do you feel you have made? Is there anything you would change? What was the methodology for including research material?" Then followed technical questions dealing with content.

Loren's answers were brilliant and given with charm and confidence, obviously forgetting he was "on the stand." The atmosphere became more relaxed. For an hour and fifteen minutes the discussion went on.

Questions over, Loren became nervous again when he and his "support group" were asked to leave the room while the professors deliberated. Dr. J. J. Roberts had a class and needed to leave early. Before doing so, however, he passed a note to Dr. Miller. Lois, curious and eager, saw a word beginning with an "s" on the note. Could it be "summa?" She wondered.

Loren was called into the room again and invited to be seated in his chair. "It is the unanimous decision of the faculty to award you the PhD degree *Summa Cum Laude*," Dr. Miller told him. Stunned, but not for long, Loren thanked them, and then said, "I think I'm going to cry." And he did! While the professors took their turns signing the document, Dr. Charlesworth opened the door and called out: "Earl...Earl—summa cum laude!" We could see through the glass door that Dr. Miller and Dr. Kathy Sakenfeld, who were seated on each side of Loren, were embracing him through tears of joy.

It was an emotional moment for all of us. Fifteen years of college and seminary studies, interrupted by two years as a Fulbright scholar in Tübingen, Germany, and one year of teaching New Testament at Kiel University in the Faculty of Theology in Germany, had come to a climax. Loren returned to Kiel September 25th to complete his six year contract. Even today, Dr. Stuckenbruck remains just "Loren" to everybody, and that is the way he likes it.

Four years after Loren received his doctorate, he was invited to speak at a number of Dead Sea Scrolls' conferences, including the one in Jerusalem, July 29—August 6, 1997. It was the 50th anniversary of the finding of the Dead Sea Scrolls, an area of Loren's expertise. While in Jerusalem, Loren decided he had to visit the Qumran caves where the Dead Sea Scrolls were found even if he had to go alone! With five jugs of water, he set out. Twice people went looking for him to no avail. Finally, after five hours and empty jugs, he stumbled into a Kibbutz where he was revived and driven back to Jerusalem almost dehydrated but *happy*!

5
Jane's Journey

One of the many times when we were present for Jane's concerts, was in February, 1990. The music teachers of Houston County, Georgia, sponsored her in concert at the Warner Robins Civic Center. The audience gasped when she walked onto the stage, in a flowing aqua gown, smiling. They gasped even more as she performed Chopin, Debussy, Rachmaninoff, Liszt, and Mozart. Jane played as though she were performing for thousands even though only a portion of the huge auditorium was filled. TV channel 13 filmed a cut to be shown on the evening news and she was invited to the studio the next morning for an interview and to play a Chopin number.

Jane's determination to be a part of the hearing world paid off. It had been a long journey. Because of her severe hearing loss, Jane knows what hopelessness means. She has had teachers give up on her because of her handicap. Then in the Waldorf School in Germany, Fraulein Gertrude Maliga, an actress, came to her aid. She became Jane's teacher, volunteering her services at school six days a week, teaching her voice control and voice projection through memorizing reams of poetry in German and English. To this day, Jane gives Fraulein Maliga credit for her good speech which is both beneficial and a handicap. When people hear her talk, it is hard for them to believe that she is deaf which places demands on Jane which are sometimes difficult to fulfill. It is beneficial, however, because it allows her to be a part of the hearing world which has indeed proved a great blessing to her and to those who have benefitted from her teaching and been blessed by her music.

In the Waldorf classroom, Jane had sat beside Werner Krauss, a top student, and copied his notes. In addition, he filled in the gaps when she did not understand material that was presented in class. Pupils in the Waldorf School made their own text books by copying material presented by teachers in the classroom and through research and then drawing pictures to illustrate the subject matter. She always dreamed that someday she would give back to other kids what she had learned.

Years later, when she moved with her husband Bob and daughter Angela to Perry, Georgia, she was hired to teach music in two public elementary schools with students totaling 800! "The principals were courageous to hire me," she said. Principal Hunt commented: "The way the kids respond to her is unusual. They show a lot of respect for her. They seem to know something isn't quite right, but they don't worry about it. We're lucky to have an unusual teacher with an extraordinary talent."

Everyone was helpful. When anything was said on intercom, someone would come from the office to explain to Jane anything that had been broadcast. Even though she could not often understand words people said, she confessed that she would read their lips and interpret the rhythm of their voices.

Jane was elected not only **Teacher of the Year** in the two schools where she taught but also **Teacher of the Year** for the county. It was an exciting moment when the teachers of Houston County met in August 1989 at the Civic Auditorium in Warner Robins and her name was called as having won this award. At first there was silence for husband Bob, also a teacher, had to use sign language to let Jane know what had happened. School Supt. Matt Arthur presented her with a dozen red roses, $500.00 from the Chamber of Commerce, $200.00 from the Board of Education, monetary and other gift certificates from stores, restaurants, dry cleaning establishment, and civic organizations. She attributes all this to teachers and others who were patient and those who did not leave her "outside" in the realm of learning. In Johnson City, Tennessee, Jane was voted **Teacher of the Year** twice and as well **Composer of the Year** twice by the Appalachian Music Teachers Association.

In 1995, Jane's husband, Robert, completed his doctoral dissertation. It was entitled: "Jane's Story: A Description of One Deaf Person's Experiences with Literacy." Since Bob's dissertation was written about Jane, she, together with her interpreter, Faye Geary, was required to sit in on Bob's defense of his dissertation at the University of Georgia at Athens. The moderator said she read the dissertation to her husband through laughter and tears, as they traveled home from Florida—laughter at Jane's description of huge pictures on the walls of the Ear, Nose, and Throat Clinic in Tübingen, especially about one picture of the inside of a purple mouth and in the back, "where," Jane said, "a funny looking thing hangs upside down waiting to drop," and tears as she read of Jane's struggle to succeed despite her hearing impairment.

6.
Dale

There was a time when Dale, though performing and teaching, was also concert master and sometimes contractor for Broadway shows in Manhattan. On one occasion he arranged for us to see "The Secret Garden" for which he was concert master and in-house contractor for the twenty-five member orchestra in the pit at St. James Theater. *Time* magazine had this to say about "The

Secret Garden:" "Vibrant and thought provoking to look at, melodic and poignant to hear, blessed with a dazzling 11-year-old star, 'The Secret Garden' is rarest of entertainments...a story fascinating to children, sophisticated and stimulating for adults." We loved it!

We were also thrilled when, in June, 1997, we were just starting out to church, when Dale phoned and said he was in the NBC studio in N.Y. and would be on in a few minutes. He was concert master and contractor for the Broadway show, "Dr. Jekyll and Mr. Hyde," and he and five other string players were accompanying two singers from the show to advertise it. John Stuckenbruck, his cousin in Springfield, MA, not knowing that Dale would be "on," recognized him on the clip. We went on to church that morning on cloud nine for we had seen our son.

7.
New Arrivals

It was during the Christmas season that great expectations were fulfilled in the birth of two grandsons, five days apart. We hurried north to Long Island and Princeton to be present for the two events.

Back in Tennessee, we had received a phone call from Heawon and Dale. "The baby's coming," they said. We were expecting the call. Happily, we packed our car and drove to Hicksville, Long Island. It was 5:30 p.m. when we arrived. Heawon was waiting. The table was set and baked salmon was served. Dale was playing a Haydn concert at St. James Cathedral in Manhattan. It was nearly midnight before he came bounding up the steps to greet us before going to bed.

And so, unto Dale and Heawon was born a son on Long Island December 31, 1990, on the sixth day of Christmas, on the night of the "Blue Moon," when, at midnight, one second was added because the earth was slowing down. They named the baby Orin Lee and called him Orin, the name of his great grandfather Stuckenbruck. It is also significant that in Korean Tradition, the same syllable is used on the end of children's names in a family. Dale and Haewon's daughter was called Car**in** thus Or**in**'s name fits that tradition.

Three years after Orin's birth, Erin Elsie was born at 12:20 p.m., April 12, 1994, at North Shore Hospital in Manhassett, N.Y. Else (Else Mosalkow) was the name of the "German grandmother by proxie," of our children. Three-year-old Orin was glad he now had a sister on earth, for Carin had gone to heaven. There was joy, joy, joy as we shared the news with other family members.

Dale was not the only one to have additions to his family that Christmas season. Unto Loren and Lois was born a son January 5, 1991, in Princeton, New Jersey, on the eleventh day of Christmas, and they named him Johann Richard David, and called him Hanno. Richard David was the name of his grandfather Loban. It was later learned that great grandmother Loban's father had the name Richard David and he was also born January 5! Another coincidence is that Hanno arrived on his great grandparents' 62nd wedding anniversary. The name "Hanno" is mentioned as a character in Thomas Mann's book, *Budden-Brooks,* an insight into the life of young Hanno. While we were celebrating God's wonderful Gift, JESUS, we were also rejoicing for the "gifts" of new life in our family. We marveled how God sends little ones "readymade" in detail (Ps. 139:13–18).

8.
Awards!

October 1991, we drove to Tulsa, Oklahoma, to be present for the convention of the General Assembly of the Christian Churches, Disciples of Christ. While there, we attended a "Walker

Lecture" by Dr. William Baird, of Brite College of the Bible, sponsored by the European Evangelistic Society, on October 30. It happened to be Earl's 75th birthday. A big surprise awaited him. Arthur Hanna, of the Pension Fund of the Christian Churches, stepped forward, made a little speech, and invited me to pin the Honored Minister's Pin on a lapel of Earl's suit jacket—an unexpected treasure.

Six years later, we received letters from Robert Shaw and the Christian Theological Seminary, in sequence, giving instructions about the conferral of doctoral degrees. I had not noticed that it was worded in the plural. Rereading the letters, I was shocked to see that I was included and tried to figure out why. In my mind, Earl was a great person and scholar and I believed that he deserved any honor bestowed upon him. Then, for the first time, I came to recognize how blended our lives were. It was special that the committee making the decisions had graciously included me.

Later, on April 22, 1997, Dr. Richard and Becky Phillips helped sponsor the planting of a Red Oak in our honor on the campus of Christian Theological Seminary.

At the May 19, 1996, commencement of Christian Theological Seminary, nee Butler School of Religion, Earl and I were granted Honorary Doctor of Divinity Degrees. The citation read that we had made significant contributions in education, evangelism, and humanitarian service as foreign missionaries. Our particular mission was to witness, in a European university setting, faith and fellowship in Jesus Christ for the sake of both Christian unity and evangelism, which is not dependent on the authority of any particular denomination, only upon obedience to Jesus Christ.

In February 1997, nine months after we had been granted these honorary degrees, the phone rang and Earl and I answered simultaneously on two phones. "You're a winner," a person at the Johnson City Press told us. "A winner of what?" Earl wanted to know. Afterwards, I showed him a letter I had written entitled

"The Champion of My Life" for a contest sponsored by the Johnson City Press and revealed that I had written about him! The inspiration to enter the contest had come as I reviewed the multiple poems he had written for me which I had mounted on a wall in my laundry room! They had helped dispel the drudgery of washing and ironing. Below is the letter I wrote:

> "The **Champion of my life**" is my husband Earl for more than fifty years! This thoughtful, kind, compassionate, humble, diligent encourager has commended himself not only to his immediate family and kin near and far, but also to people on all echelons of life—from scholars to the marginalized, to people in Germany where he started an Institute for the Study of Christian Origins and a Christian Church, to local colleges, churches and a multitude of others in this community and across the nation. For his 80th birthday celebration in October, he was showered with 'gifts of words': His children spoke of bonding with him while watching in wonder a double rainbow together, while taking walks together, while listening to and making beautiful music together, and etc. Students he taught still seek him out for discussions and to say, 'Thank you.' He serves as elder and on the missions committee at his church. He always has an encouraging word to say, and often a humorous comment, to those in a Piccadilly line, in grocery stores or wherever he meets people in the community. Excuse my pride, but sharing life with my champion has been/is a precious, ever-growing experience.

The following is an announcement in the paper regarding this award:

> Johnson Citian Ottie Mearl Stuckenbruck said she almost called to withdraw from the essay contest, thinking,

erroneously, that nominees had to be those 'who had changed the world' and not, as she wrote, the 'thoughtful, kind, compassionate, humble, diligent, encourager' of her essay.

Earl Stuckenbruck, Ottie Mearl's husband of nearly fifty-three years, was, however, just the type of champion the contest sought to spotlight. As a missionary, he had spread the Gospel across the globe. As a father, he shared the brilliance of a double rainbow with his children. As a husband, he offered his wife an abundance of love. And, Ottie Mearl wrote, to strangers 'in a Picadilly line, in grocery stores or wherever, he always provides an encouraging word or humorous comment.'

"Well, I can't say that she's concealed this all these 53 years," Earl said last week at his Johnson City home, as his wife looked on admiringly. "No, I've known that she was at least tolerating me." More than that, Ottie Mearl said: "Well, you know, when couples are first married, they think they are in love—and they are, but I know I love him more now than when we were first married."

"I think that's true," her husband interjected, "because the qualities of people are not just out front at first. You observe people, don't you, when the trials come and the difficulties come, and how they handle all these things. I think you appreciate one another more after you've gone through things than when you've just been on a honeymoon." As if on cue, Ottie Mearl finished her husband's words, "We've had a lot of things to think about, pray about, and overcome," she said, turning to Earl and smiling.

Host for the awards ceremony will be Tom Hodge, editorial director for the Johnson City Press.

At the May 27, 2001, Emmanuel School of Religion's commencement, Earl and I were granted the James A. Garfield Award, ESR's highest honor. A definition of this award reads as follows: "Candidates for The James A. Garfield Award have rendered noteworthy service to the Church, whether it be through administration, benevolence, scholarship, pastoral ministry, or other forms of service."—*The Envoy.*

In the citations read by Dr. Bruce Shields, it was stated that we had been commissioned by the European Evangelistic Society to seek out a university on the continent of Europe, after World War II, for an academic and evangelistic base. We settled in Tübingen, Germany, where we established a church, "Christliche Gemeinde," and an academic theological institute, "Das Institut Zur Erforschung Des Urchristentums."

Earl's response: "We are honored to receive the James A Garfield Award in behalf of those who initiated, encouraged, and sustained the mission of the European Evangelistic Society in Tübingen, Germany."

My response: "**This is a proud day.** But Longfellow was right when he wrote: 'tis not in titles nor in rank that matters.' We all here today know that reproducing the life of Jesus Christ, life's finest, sweetest, biggest challenge, is what counts. We just have to find our niche to do it. Thank you for this award. We accept it with thankfulness for all the rope-holders while we were serving in Europe. Some of you are in the audience today. You are the heroes!"

9.
Celebrations

And there were not only awards. There were celebrations too. Take for instance, our golden wedding anniversary! Earl and I had been married 50 years, June 1, 1994, and it was time to celebrate. Dr. Dick Phillips, Fine Arts Chair at First Christian Church in Johnson City, made arrangements for a family community concert to be held at the church. Earl Lee and Lavanne came from North Carolina, Jane, Bob and Angela from Georgia,

GOLDEN NUPTIAL SERENADE
MAY 22, 1994, JOHNSON CITY, TENNESSEE

Loren performs Chopin

Dale, Earl Lee, Loren & Jane play "The Lord is My Shepherd" by Crimond on recorders

Amy plays Bach prelude

Lois was helpful organizer, decision-maker, and general hostess.

Lavanne played "Tribute" on her accordion.

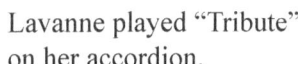

Dale & Heawon perform Mendelssohn & Wieniawski for violin & piano also a Korean Folk song on musical saw.

Bob sings "Elixer of Love" by Donizetti, "If With All Thy Heart" from ELIJAH.

Jane plays Moszkowski, Rachmaniof & Schubert.

Angela played a classical medley, selection of Show Tunes and a hymn.

Dale and Heawon from New York, and Loren and Lois from England. A niece, Amy Langner, organist, came from Alabama. All were participating musicians. Featured were the organ, accordion, piano, harp, recorders, violin, vocal numbers and (of course) the saw.

After the concert, Dr. George Kehler, Hungarian pianist and professor at East Tennessee State University, wrote: "For one family to be made up of so many highly accomplished musicians is more than exceptional. This entire presentation reflected, in addition to the talent, the enormous discipline and dedication of the performers." This was one of the happiest times of our lives—having all family members together and with relatives and friends who came from afar. It was, indeed, a perfect serenade for our 50th wedding anniversary.

Two years later, on October 30, 1996, Earl became an octogenarian and there was another celebration. It was important to have something to talk about that has meaning, Earl told us, rather than simply a time to enjoy cake and ice cream together.

And so an invitation was sent to close friends to come to our home, suggesting that our conversation revolve around the relationship of trust to faith/belief.

My 75th birthday celebration came five years later. For the past few years, Earl had been in and out of hospitals with cancer, knee replacements, and for sundry other health issues. I stayed with him and slept nights in the furnished lean-back chairs by his bed. We were at the Medical Center on my 75th birthday. We had planned that it would be "just another day." However, in the afternoon, there was a surprise party in Earl's hospital room. Mignon Holben, David and Pam Holben, Grandmother Ruth Holben, and Dr. Henry and Em Webb came with cake, drinks, balloons, Italian candy, and set up a party! They even had a camera to capture the memory. Our friends had gone to a great deal of effort to try and make me feel my age! Precious people!

Five years passed when it was time for another celebration. I think my family wanted to prove to our friends and *me* that I was turning eighty! Gerda Schauer, in Tübingen, Germany, wrote that people in the church there never knew how old I was, and wondered.

Unknown to me, Dale and Heawon contacted some forty families and friends, mostly from Butler University School of Religion days, in our area, with the help of Harry and Dorothy Young and Leonard and Thelma Wymore, and invited them to a celebration dinner in the lounge at Appalachian Christian Village Towers, residence of Harry and Dorothy and others. I knew there was a secret happening, but I didn't know what.

After church, April 28, I was ushered to a party at The Towers, a part of Appalachian Christian Village. The lounge was beautifully decorated by Jane. Angela was the gopher and door hostess. Heawon was in charge of the food—shrimp, beef and pork kababs and rice—colorful and delicious! Dale and Bob were her helpers. Orin and Erin served a birthday cake.

We moved from tables to comfortable sofas for a program. Earl Lee was MC. Jane gave a speech about our journey together in life and performed on the piano. Eleven-year-old Orin performed all three movements of a Vivaldi Sonata for violin, with Heawon accompanying. Eight-year-old Erin sang several verses of "Praise Him, Praise Him" while Jane interpreted with sign language. A wonderful letter was read by Earl Lee from Loren and Lois in Durham, England. Then Dale, violinist, and Heawon, pianist, thrilled the audience with a Tchaikovsky (a favorite composer of Earl) piece. Dale and Heawon had made all the plans from afar, and it was amazing how well they carried them out locally. I am forever indebted to my family for their love and thoughtfulness.

Joint birthdays were also a cause for celebrations. At Thanksgiving, we would celebrate the shared birthdays of Earl, Dale, and Maya Rheinhardt Milligan. It had become the custom for Maya to come from California to celebrate with Earl, a practice that was begun in Germany many years before. This time, she brought her son, David. We reminisced, and each person told Earl how his life had had an influence on them. Precious were the words of all to be remembered.

Family reunions, too, were a part of our lives as we grew older. We have been able to attend a number of the family reunions on my father's side of the family at Lawley, Alabama. There was always a program and dinner on the ground at Tabernacle Church. Mary Ella Moore Henderson, a cousin, planned the programs for many years, succeeded by her daughter, Sadie Evelyn. It has been our privilege to become re-acquainted with many relatives we had not seen during our twenty-three years overseas. In addition, we were able to be present at a couple of family reunions of my Wallace relatives on my birth mother's side, hosted by Faye, my mother's sister, in Cardova, Alabama.

Earl's first cousins, Dr. Louis Chenette and Dr. Eugene Chenette, planned a family reunion, August 1998, remembering Earl's mother's family, in the Corbin area of Kentucky where Earl's mother, May Chestnut Stuckenbruck, was born. The group met for a banquet at Kastle Inn, Mt. Vernon, Ky. A program included Earl playing the musical saw. He played a piece composed by his uncle, Ed Chenette, titled "Love's Day," accompanied by Sue Chenette, wife of first cousin, Steve. Steve and Sue taught in the music department at Toronto University.

Sunday, August 10, Chesnut (Chenette) relatives gathered in a little church in Renfro Valley, Ky., possibly one in which our ancestors had preached. On this occasion, Earl was the preacher. He talked about "Family in the Perspective of God." Eugene Chenette presided. Jonathan Chenette, Earl's second cousin, led the singing and we sang one of his own compositions.

Chapter Seventeen
At Home and Abroad

1
Inauguration of the Walker Lectures

An inaugural dinner for the European Evangelistic Society to introduce the Walker Lectures was held at the McCormick Dining Hall on the Milligan College campus, April 8, 1988. The occasion was to honor Dr. Dean E. Walker, long time president of the EES, president emeritus of Milligan College, and former president and founder of Emmanuel Christian Seminary, nee Emmanuel School of Religion. For a year, Earl had worked hard to raise funds for an endowment of twenty thousand dollars for lectures to be given every four years for the conventions of the World Convention, every two years for the conventions of the General Assemblies of the Disciples of Christ, and every year for the conventions of the North American Christian Convention. In addition to honoring Dr. Walker, it was a means of encouraging Christian unity of the different conventions, of creating awareness that the EES exists, and of making possible lectures by some of the finest scholars in the three movements of our people. Dr. Fred Thompson, president of Emmanuel School of Religion, was the inaugural speaker. Unfortunately, four days before the inauguration dinner for the lectures, Dr. Walker died. The memorial service was held at Hopwood Christian Church on the Milligan College campus.

2.
Faith In Practice

Faith In Practice is the title of a book—studies in the book of Acts— written by some of the scholars who have served on the staff of the Institute for Research in Christian Origins in Tübingen and, in addition, a contribution by a friend of the Institute, Prof. Dr. Otto Betz. Dr. Robert Shaw, president of the EES, wrote: "The practice of the early Church, its way of life in the world, has been a common interest for all the scholars who have worked at the Institute." The editors, David A. Fiensy and William D. Howden, commented: "It is our desire, as editors and authors, that these essays not only enhance our understanding of the early Church, but help guide the Church in its practice of faith today." *Faith In Practice,* printed by College Press, is a festschrift in our honor, and the first copy was presented to us at the North American Christian Convention in Indianapolis, July, 1995.

3.
History of the EES by Some of the Original Cast

May 1996, Robert Shaw arranged for the annual meeting of the EES board to meet at the Christian Theological Seminary in Indianapolis, Indiana. Members were invited to speak in chapel to students, faculty and guests about the history of the EES. The messages were videotaped for the school's permanent files which were stored in the library. Actually, professors at CTS were founders of the EES and had invited us to go out under their auspices. And so the history of the EES is also a part of the history of CTS.

Several of those who spoke had been with the organization from the beginning or were students at Butler. Earl told about our entrance into Europe, finding a location for the work, and the founding of the Institute for Research in Christian Origins. My part was to tell about the Student Volunteer Chapter on campus at Butler School of Religion which Virginia Beven and I had started that had generated interest in foreign missions. The soil was fertile. In the wake of Pearl Harbor, there was an urgency to take Christ to the world. Also, I talked about the beginning of the Christian Church in Tübingen and the German American Women's Club which I started with the help of a couple of German ladies, Dora Reich and Hilde Achtstetter. Others spoke as well. It was wonderful to be on the CTS campus again, reminiscent of how Earl and I had met, of our love for each other, and of our mutual passion for missions.

4.
EES and Eberhard-Karls Universität Sponser Symposium

Perhaps it can be said that the presence of the EES in Tübingen reached its apex in 2009 when a symposium, jointly sponsored by the Institute zur Erforschung des Urchristentums and Eberhard-Karls Universität, took place in an old stone building on campus. Seventeen international scholars presented their Research on the Septuagint, the Bible of the first Christians, and Christian Origins. Dr. Scott Caulley, Director of the Institute, and his wife, Cherie, invited me to be their guest for the occasion of a double celebration: the 60th anniversary of our arrival in Tübingen to create a base for the work of the EES and the symposium. Dale and Heawon made the trip financially possible for me to go and also for their daughter, 16-year-old Erin, to accompany me. I was so pleased to have this experience with my granddaughter. While I was attending the symposium, she was becoming acquainted with the Waldorfschule. Later she attended the school for a semester.

Dr. Caulley, Dr. Ron Heine, former Institute Director, and Dr. Lichtenberger of the University put together what Wye Huxford, U.S.A. EES Director, describes as "an important contribution to the world of biblical scholarship for years to come." Oh, how Earl would have loved this!

Isolde Betz, a German friend, and I were among lay persons who heard the lectures and were able to follow along with manuscripts furnished by the scholars. Dr. Bruce Shields, EES president, and W.L. and Cheri Thompson were also guests from the U.S. On the closing evening when Loren, by now a N.T. professor at Princeton Theological Seminary, gave his lecture, Dr. Caulley, in lieu of our husbands, Earl Stuckenbruck and Otto Betz, who have preceded us to our heavenly home, honored Isolde Betz and me for having created a base in Tübingen sixty years ago and for making possible an Institute for Research in Christian Origins.

Chapter Eighteen
Our Family Contracts and Expands

1.
Travels

Following two years of teaching at Kiel University in Germany, Loren received an invitation to join the theological faculty at Durham University in England. They were there fifteen years. He and Lois invited Earl and me to visit them in 1995. It was wonderful to become acquainted with Daniella and Hanno, our precious grandchildren, and learn to know colleagues and friends of Lois and Loren. Getting acquainted with the university city of Durham, with its narrow streets, quaint shops, castle, and cathedral, reminded us of our beloved Tübingen. Traffic flowed on cobble stone streets where allowed, but, unlike traffic in Tübingen, it all, of course, was traveling on the "wrong" side of the road!

We found Loren and Lois and family happy and thriving in their English environment. After church on our first Sunday in Durham, we had dinner at the "high table" at St John's College where Lois worked. This was a very formal occasion. Professors with their families and guests waited in the Common Room, where hors-d'oeuvres were served, until students assembled. When we entered the dining hall, the students respectfully stood. We gathered at a table especially prepared for us. A blessing was said and all were seated. Guests were introduced. The meal was served. At the end, a benediction was given and the groups of professors filed out while the students remained standing. The professors and their guests assembled in the Common Room again for a visit before departing.

One special event we attended, among others, revealed what wonderful hostesses Loren and Lois were in formal entertaining. It was an evening spent with Dr. and Mrs. C.K. Barrett (Kingsley and Margaret). Kingsley was a retired, world renowned New Testament scholar. Prof. Martin Hengel in Tübingen had instructed the Barretts to take care of Loren and Lois in Durham.

Earl and I also traveled in the States. Wherever and whenever the Walker Lectures were held in the conventions of the three segments of the Restoration Movement, Earl and I tried to be there and usually Earl introduced the speaker. In 2001, the General Assembly was held in Kansas City, KS. In addition to attending the lecture by Dr. David Balch and other meetings, we visited with people at the European Evangelistic Society booth. An additional pleasure was visiting Kansas University in Lawrence, Earl's alma mater. He had not been back in sixty-two years! He is indebted to K.U. for a free education, having received a Summerfield Scholarship, which paid all of his expenses for four years!

2.
Farewell to Harry

Harry, Earl's only sibling, Springfield, Massachusetts, passed away January 13, 1998, at the age of eighty. He had worked in the personnel department at the home office of Massachusetts Mutual Life Insurance Co. for thirty-eight years and was assistant director. Harry was a well known civic leader in the community and served as interim minister for the United Church of Christ throughout

Western Massachusetts. He also served as a youth director at Hope Congregational Church for a number of years. At one time, he was president of the Council of Churches of Greater Springfield and of the Kiwanis Club. He and his wife, Lucille, of fifty-seven years entertained at meetings with unusual instruments such as water glasses and a saw. Harry is survived by his wife, Lucille Roach Stuckenbruck, a son, John, three grandchildren, and his brother, Earl. Dale, Heawon, Orin, and Erin represented our family at the private internment on January 15. Orin and Erin laid flowers on the casket.

But although we mourned the parting from one we loved, we rejoiced in new life added to our family. September 14, 1999, Nathan Hyam was born to Lois and Loren, in Durham, England— a precious heavenly gift, our youngest grandchild. Of course, he received a lot of TLC from his siblings, Daniella and Hanno, and we sent bundles of love.

Then in September 2, 2001, we became great grandparents when Jonathan Aaron Ashe was born to Shawn and Sabrina in Asheville, North Carolina. They called him Aaron. We drove to the hospital to see him. We pray that Aaron will have a second birth someday. (John 3:3) When he is older, I would like to tell him about one of my favorite Bible verses: John 14:23, etc. Two more great grandchildren were added March 29, 2004. Allison and Ariel, twin sisters, joined their brother, Aaron. We are thankful for three beautiful, lovable great grandchildren.

Two babes at once! How very nice,
To have such sweetness given twice;
Four little feet instead of two,
Four little hands to guide and do;
Two little hearts to guard and keep
And teach a lay-me-down to-sleep.
Four starry eyes to look into
When once-upon-a-times are through;
A pair of hurts to kiss and tell
To never mind, 'twill soon be well.'

And two tight hugs to let you see
How much "I love you" means to me.
To watch one tiny life unfold
Is worth a miser's pot of gold,
But seeing two go hand in hand
I think must be the grandest grand!
        By Jessie Marie Franklin.

Dale, Haewan, Ottie Mearl, Lois, Daniella, Earl Lee
Hanno, Orin, Erin, Earl, Loren, Nathan, Jane & Angela

3.
Earl Released from Earth to his Heavenly Home

Earl's health continued to deteriorate—prostate cancer, heart issues. But we were able occasionally to visit Jane and Bob in Perry, GA. and, of course, attend church. Eventually, he became house bound.

Finally, we called in Hospice, and for a year and a half he had excellent care. We were blessed with weekly visits from church members who came with communion.

October 13, 2008, at one o'clock in the morning, Earl, my love and inestimable champion, passed away. I called Earl Lee who was sleeping next door and he contacted Hospice. It was wonderful that Hospice took over all the necessary details of the moment. We appreciated the fact that the men who came for Earl from the Appalachian Funeral Home showed their respect by wearing suits and ties.

A memorial service was held for Earl at First Christian in Johnson City, with Drs. Tim Wallingford and Don Jeanes officiating, and with colleagues and friends, Drs. Bill Gwaltney, Bob Wetzel, Aaron Wymer, Fred Norris, Richard Phillips, Bruce Shields and Frank Smith participating. We continue to sense his presence, along with the constant presence of Jesus, as we live out our lives.

4.
Farewell to Earl Lee

With a diploma from the Aubrey Willis School showing the completion of a course in Piano Tuning, Regulating and Repairing, an apprenticeship with a famous piano tuner technician, Clayton Harmon, a Certificate of Recognition as an All Steinway School Technical Partner, a registered Piano Technician certificate and testimonials of his work by institutions and individuals, Earl Lee felt that he had reached the peak of his profession.

Then tragedy struck. Two days before Thanksgiving, 2011, he was diagnosed with lung cancer. He called me to his bedside at the VA for a private meeting and explained that he was told that he had days, maybe weeks to live. We prayed together and asked our Heavenly Father to help us through this, and He did. Earl Lee was allowed to come home for Thanksgiving and he and his friend, Phil Hendrix, baked the turkey which Earl Lee had traditionally done. At the dinner table were guests, Leonard and Thelma Wymore, Jackie Scribner, Dale and Phil Hendrix. It was suggested that each person tell about blessings he/she had received during the past year. When it came Earl Lee's turn, he stood, clicked his glass and made a farewell speech!

For the next two months, Earl Lee was a patient at the VA hospital and was treated with special care. Nurses and others would come by just to say, "Thank you for serving our country!" Phil Hendrix came from Asheville and was constantly at his bedside. Maya came from California. Sadie Evelyn came from Georgia. Urte, a friend, came from Germany. Lois came from Princeton. Connie came from South Carolina. All these people came from a distance to help.

We will also never forget how members of Grandview Christian Church ministered to his needs and ours during that difficult time, especially the minister, Aaron Wymer. January 26, 2012, three days after his 62nd birthday, with family and his friend, Phil, at his bedside, Earl Lee, made the sign for "I love you" in sign language and passed away. It was so obvious that God loved him, and that there was a response to that love. His siblings, Dale, Loren, and Jane, prepared a beautiful memorial service for Earl Lee, with Dr. Aaron Wymer officiating. At this writing, three years later, we still get calls for his piano tuning from people unaware of his death. Gone but not forgotten!

Chapter 19
Still Walking With Jesus

1.
My Ninetieth Birthday

April 29, 2012, my two sisters, Gertha and Inell, together with their daughters, Sherry, Sandi and Amy, drove up from Randolph, Anniston, Stanton and Guntersville, Alabama, to celebrate the "age event." It was my ninetieth birthday! They arrived mid-afternoon.

Gertha, Ottie Mearl, and Inell

We watched a video of Earl Lee's memorial service, and then the group excused themselves. The next time I saw them, they had showered, washed and dried their hair, and donned their Sunday best. It was time to celebrate with a meal at a restaurant of my choice. Could anything be better than Chinese food? Not far away was an appropriate place. Jane and Angela joined us. A couple of nice waitresses at the restaurant set up a table in a not-so-fancy but adequate room for privacy. Our plates piled high with you-name-it food to last for twelve hours, we enjoyed conversation and fellowship. That done, we returned home to a surprise party! Not only was there entertainment, each one brought a gift. One brought Amazing Grace chimes which continue to tinkle when the wind blows, reminding me of my precious family's presence on that memorable occasion. Journals are now filled with events of following days and months and a little Willow Tree box, signed with "an embrace of comfort and love," has a special place on my dresser. In addition, there were home grown vegetables in fruit jars given by one who grows her own garden. All so special! My guests had an agenda. Now it was time to sleep.

Morning came and the focus was on their returning home, but not before a waffle breakfast. Less than twenty-four hours from the time of their arrival, they were packed and on their way home again. Unforgettable! It had been worth living 90 years to have this happen.

Birthday celebrations were not over, however. Lois and Heawon conceived the idea of a very special event to celebrate my 90th birthday, but at a later date, by hosting, together with Loren and Dale and their families, a special sit-down dinner-party with friends. A not-so-easy task! Loren was out of the country, teaching at Hebrew University in Jerusalem, and would not be home in

Princeton until June. Lois and Nathan decided to join him during the last six weeks of his stay. Although some arrangements were made in advance of their going, much of the final preparations were actually made from Jerusalem, with the help of Heawon in New York. Jane made the place cards. It was a big undertaking!

The party took place in McCormick Dining Hall at Milligan College and was catered and served by Milligan kitchen personnel. Loren was MC for the event and began the evening with prayer. Lois had created a table game for conversation while we ate. The people at each table were given fifty questions. If they could answer them, they would know the story of my life. Trudy Tait's table knew the most answers to the questions. She had read some of my life story! She is, actually, one of my favorite authors and had written a poem for the occasion.

After enjoying table fellowship, a cake with a floral candle, measuring 1 1/2" across the top, was set before me. Loren lit it and a number of surrounding small candles raised up around the larger one shining their little lights. The birthday song was sung, and we all waited to see what would happen next, for obviously that candle wasn't finished. After several seconds, with nothing happening, we were beginning to relax and guests who had gathered round were returning to their seats. Suddenly, there was an explosion. A large beautiful flame leaped into the air from the candle. The cake was served, crowning a delicious meal.

The evening was not over. The special part was yet to come. There could be no Stuckenbruck party without music. Dale had put together a program. He told us about his new hobby of collecting singing stones and performed on his violin and musical saw. Erin, Orin and Hanno sang as a trio. Orin and Hanno played their guitars. Hanno played a classical solo on his guitar. Nathan read a greeting he had composed. Great grandchildren, Aaron and Allison, played a piece on their recorders. A couple, Dr. Louis and Emily Chenette, who had come from Indianapolis, Indiana, felt right at home. Before retirement he had been head of the Arthur Jordan Conservatory of Music at Butler University. He was Earl's first cousin. Music is a family gift.

Sitting down with family and friends for an evening of fellowship and fun was the most special gift one could imagine. Thank you, dear family. UNFORGETTABLE!!

2.
Into the Future

At the same time that Lois was planning the party, she was packing for their move to Munich, Germany, August 1. Loren had been teaching at Princeton Theological Seminary and now he was invited to join the theological faculty at Ludwig-Maximiliens—Universitaet. At this point, three years later, they are well settled, and Loren says that he has freedom to pursue his interest in "the part Jewish tradition has to play in the shaping of early Christianity—the exploration of early Christianity through the New Testament and the traditions that shaped it has huge implications for living out of a Christian life of faith, a faith that is at once visionary, challenging, and realistic, without being under illusions about what it means to be a Christian." Daniella remains in the States; Nathan is with his parents while Hanno is at King's College, London, majoring in music—conducting.

Dale and Heawon are still in N.Y., teaching at Post University and privately, giving solo and chamber group recitals, Dale acting as music director at a Waldorf School and more. Orin has completed a degree in visual arts at N. Y. University Visual Arts Center. Erin is a student at Bard University.

Jane lives in Johnson City, Tennessee, where she teaches piano, gives lectures to homeschoolers, and cares for her daughter, Angela, who has been ill for some time.

3.
I am ready!

My life journey, from my birth in Telladega forest in Alabama to the present, has been one of striving, adventure, and service. It is hard to believe that I am now over ninety years of age. I continue to feel young.

If our lives, as recorded in these pages, have seemed to be perfect, they were not. We experienced heartaches, changes, blunders, disappointments, and desperate situations, but, in my opinion, it helps no one to reveal the negatives that injure and disrupt families. When troubles came, we knew we had an advocate, Jesus, who gave us hope and we could face the future.

The recognition that Jesus Christ, my constant companion, is the same yesterday, today, and forever, has helped me keep my focus and feel secure on my journey.

I am 93 years young, have a busy life, but am waiting. I know the close of life will come. I am ready!

Books by
Trudy Harvey Tait

Biographies
Three in Love

Novels
The Velvet Curtain
Behind the Velvet Curtain
Escaping the Velvet Curtain
Love Me & Let Me Go

Poems
Reflections

Children's
Licky the Singing Mouse

Obtainable through any bookstore
or at
www.harveycp.com

www.ingramcontent.com/pod-product-compliance
Lightning Source LLC
LaVergne TN
LVHW011416080426
835512LV00005B/85